Rubem Alves

Transparencies of eternity

Translated by Jovelino and Joan Ramos

CONVIVIUMPRESS

SERIES SAPIENTIA

2010

Transparencies of eternity
© Rubem Alves

http://www.conviviumpress.com
sales@conviviumpress.com
ventas@conviviumpress.com
convivium@conviviumpress.com

7661 NW 68th St, Suite 108,
Miami, Florida 33166. USA.
Phone: +1 (786) 8669718

Edited by Rafael Luciani
Translated by Jovelino and Joan Ramos
Revision assisted by Margaret Wilde
Designed by Eduardo Chumaceiro d'E
Series: *Sapientia*

ISBN: 978-1-934996-19-5

Convivium Press
Miami 2010

Transparencies of eternity

*'What would we be without the help
of things that don't exist?*
PAUL VALÉRY

*God exists, even when he is not.
But the Devil doesn't need to exist in order to be…*
RIOBALDO

Contents

Introduction PAGE *14*
Our Father… Our Mother PAGE *16*

PART ONE
The Nameless One and the Mystery PAGE *19*

1
Does God exist? PAGE *21*

2
Without accounting PAGE *27*

3
The child God PAGE *33*

4
The stained glass window PAGE *39*

5
Dear God, cure me of being a grownup! PAGE *45*

PART TWO
Gestures and Words PAGE 49

ℳ

1
The Baptized One PAGE 51

ℳ

2
Prayer PAGE 55

ℳ

3
Promises PAGE 59

ℳ

4
What I love in the Church PAGE 63

PART THREE

Fears PAGE 69

1

Hell PAGE 71

2

On the salvation of my soul PAGE 75

3

Again, about Hell PAGE 79

4

Petrus PAGE 83

PART FOUR

Tranquility PAGE 87

1

Tending sheep PAGE 89

2

Angels PAGE 93

3

Corpus Christi PAGE 97

4

Laudate Pueri PAGE 101

PART FIVE

Beauty PAGE *107*

1
The magi PAGE *109*

2
Outside beauty there is no salvation PAGE *115*

3
The bet PAGE *121*

Copyright permissions PAGE *130*

Introduction

I lived for many years in this country running away from the military dictatorship. From those times I cherish many precious memories of loyal friends and the beauty of nature. As for the latter, what impressed me most was autumn. Autumn is like old age, which is the season in which I find myself now.

Mine was an academic education. However, there came a time when I ceased to find enjoyment in writing for my peers. I began to write for children and ordinary people, playing with humor and poetry. That's what the following short texts are all about. They are like snapshots, rather than reasoning. I don't want to prove anything. I just want to portray. There is a thread that assembles them as pearls in a necklace. Yet each text is a complete unit. Through them I try to say what I have come to feel about the sacred. I don't ask the readers to agree with me. I only ask that they permit themselves to promenade through unknown woods. «The woods are lovely, dark and deep…». What really matters is not what I write, but what you will think when provoked by what I write.

Saudade is a word I often use. I believe it is the foundation of my poetic and religious thinking. Translators with expertise in several languages say that there is no precise synonym for it in other languages. It is a feeling close to nostalgia. But it is not nostalgia. Nostalgia is pure sadness without an object. Nostalgia has no face. Whereas *saudade* is always *saudade* «of» a scenario, a face, a scene, a time. The Brazilian poet Chico Buarque wrote a song about *saudade*, in which he says that «*saudade* is a piece of me wrenched out of me, *it's to straighten up the room of the son who just died*». It is the presence of an absence.

I'll be quoting the names of several poets and writers that you probably don't know. It doesn't matter. To enjoy a beautiful piece of music one doesn't need to know the name of the composer. As in the case of music, a poem is beautiful simply because it is beautiful, and not because of who wrote it.

I hope to count on your company until the end.

RUBEM ALVES, Brazil, 2003

Our Father… Our Mother

Father… Mother… of tender eyes,
I know that you are invisible in all things.
May your name be sweet to me, the joy of my world.
Bring us the good things that give you pleasure:
a garden, fountains,
children,
bread and wine,
tender gestures, hands without weapons,
bodies hugging each other…
I know you want to meet my deepest wish,
the one whose name I forgot… but you never forget.
Bring about your wish that I may laugh.
May your wish be enacted in our world,
as it throbs inside you.
Grant us contentment in today's joys:
bread, water, sleep…
May we be free from anxiety.
May our eyes be as tender to others
as yours to us.
Because,
if we are vicious,
we will not receive your kindness.
And help us
that we may not be deceived by evil wishes.
And deliver us
from the ones who carry death inside their eyes.
Amen.

Part One

The Nameless One and the Mystery

Does God exist?

From time to time someone asks me if I believe in God. I remain silent, since anything I might say would be misunderstood. The problem lies in a simple verb whose sense is thought to be understood by everybody: *to believe.* Even without seeing these things, I believe that a mountain called the Himalayas does exist, and I believe in a star called Alpha Centauri, and I believe that inside the kitchen cabinet there is a string of onions. If I answered the question by saying that I believe in God, I would be placing God in the same rank as a mountain, a star and an onion; namely, one thing among others, with no concern about which would be the greatest.

That was how the nineteenth-century Brazilian poet Casimiro de Abreu believed in God, and we children had to memorize his poem in school:

I remember!... I was a child

...the sea was roaring

And raising aloft its proud back,

It flung the white spume against the quiet sky.

And I said in that moment to my mother:
«What a fierce orchestra! What an insane fury!
What else can be greater than the ocean,
What else can be stronger than the wind?»
Turning her gaze to the sky, and smiling,
My mother answered: «A being that we can't see.
He is greater than the sea that makes us fearful,
And stronger than the typhoon, child: he is God!»

Rhythms and rhymes are dangerous because they often make us mix bad reasoning with bad music. Apart from the rhythm and rhymes, the argument of the poet is as follows: God is «a big thing» that blows like fierce winds, and a big sea that is far more fearsome than this one. Well, I admit that such a «big thing» may exist. But no reasoning can make me love it. On the contrary, what I really want is for it to be far away from me! Who would like to live in the midst of a tempest while sailing through a terrifying sea? Not I.

It is necessary to understand, once and for all, that *to believe in God* is not worth a broken penny. Please, don't be angry with me. Rather, be angry with the apostle James, who wrote in his sacred epistle: «You believe that God is one; you do well. Even the demons believe —and shudder (James 2:19)». In other words, the apostle is saying that the demons are in a better situation than we are, since they not only believe but also shudder. Do you shudder when you hear the name of God? I doubt it. If you did, you would not repeat it so often, for fear of catching malaria.

While writing this page I am listening to Beethoven's «Appassionata», the same sonata that Lenin could listen to all day long, without getting tired of it. Its effect was such that he feared being magically transformed into joy and love, feelings incompatible with revolutionary needs (which explains why political activists, by and large, do not favor classical music). If I could hold a conversation with my dog and ask him: «Do you believe in the "Appassionata"?» he would answer: «Absolutely. Do you think I'm deaf? I can hear it. By the way, this noise is interfering with my sleep».

But I, unlike my dog, feel like crying because of its beauty. Its beauty has taken over my body and made my hair stand on end: beauty has become flesh.

Of course, I know that the sonata's existence is ephemeral. After a few minutes there will be only silence. It will live in me as memory. That is the pattern of existence that objects of love take: not as the mountain, the star and the onion, but as *saudade*. Then I will think that a way must be found for the sonata to rise from its death.

I read again and again the poems of Cecília Meireles, the Brazilian Emily Dickinson. But why, when once should be enough? Why, when I know by heart the words I am reading again? It is because the soul never tires of beauty. Beauty is a thing that makes the body tremble. There are scenes described by her that I know will last forever. Or, inversely, because they lasted eternally, she described them.

> The sunset is the calmness of heaven
> with its clouds in parallel formations
> and a final color penetrating the trees
> reaching out to the birds.
> It is the curve of pigeons over the roof tops,
> the crowing of roosters and turtle doves, far away;
> and, even farther away, the unveiling of white stars,
> still unshining.

What a fragile existence a poem has, more so than the mountain, the star, and the onion. Poems are simply words that depend on someone to write, read and recite them. Yet, words do to my body what the whole universe cannot do.

I once had dinner with a wealthy businessman who believed in God, but could not understand the reason for the picture of Cecília Meireles, an aged woman, on one of the bills of the Brazilian currency. A picture of Xuxa would have fared much better. (Xuxa is a pretty blond singer...). Indeed Xuxa is more «real» than Cecília was. Her photos are everywhere, everybody knows about her, and she is rich... Cecília, on the contrary, is an ethereal being, similar to the clouds at sunset, to the sea foam, to the flight of birds. Yet, I know that her poems will live forever. Because they are beautiful.

Beauty is a volatile entity —it touches the skin and quickly vanishes.

What we refer to with the name of God is like that: a great, huge Emptiness that encompasses the whole beauty of the universe. If the glass were not empty, we wouldn't drink water from it. If the mouth were not empty, we wouldn't eat fruit with it. If the womb were not empty, life wouldn't grow in it. If the sky were not empty, birds, clouds and kites wouldn't fly in it.

Riobaldo is the name of the hero of «Grande Sertão-Veredas», maybe the greatest of all Brazilian novels, written by João Guimarães Rosa. Riobaldo is a rude man, living far away, in wild, savage prairies. And he has a wild wisdom, knowing much about God and the Devil ... His way of speaking is strange and difficult to understand. This is what he says: «God does not exist? It is impossible! Because God exists there will always be hope, a miracle is always possible and the world makes sense. God exists even when he is not. But the Devil does not need to exist in order to be —if we know that he does not exist, that is when he takes possession of everything».

Thus, daring to use the ontology of Riobaldo, I can affirm that God has to exist. There is too much beauty in the universe, and beauty cannot be lost. God is a bottomless Emptiness, an infinite wooden trough, who wanders through the universe picking and gathering up all the beauties and guaranteeing that none will be lost, and saying that all that was loved and lost will return, and be repeated. God exists to soothe *saudade*.

Therefore I can answer the question asked of me. Of course I believe in God, the same way I believe in the colors of the sunset, the same way I believe in the perfume of the myrtle, the same way I believe in the beauty of the sonata, the same way I believe in the joy of a child at play, the same way I believe in the beauty of the gaze that falls silently upon me. All these are so fragile, so non-existing, but they make me cry. And if something makes me cry, it is sacred. It is a piece of God. The poet Valéry said: «What would we be without the help of things that don't exist?».

2

Without accounting

Walt Whitman was inspired by a spider.

«A noiseless patient spider,
I mark'd where on a little promontory it stood isolated,
Mark'd how to explore the vacant vast surrounding,
It launch'd forth filament, filament, filament, out of itself,
Ever unreeling down, ever tirelessly speeding them.
And you O my soul where you stand,
Surrounded, detached, in measureless oceans of space,
Ceaselessly musing, venturing, throwing, seeking the spheres to connect them,
Till the bridge you will need be form'd, till the ductile anchor hold,
Till the gossamer thread you fling catch somewhere, O my soul».

A spider! A metaphor of ourselves. As I write I am a spider. The gossamer threads are the words I launch forth, out of myself… My cobweb is my text. But I left two threads dangling…

The first thread came from the body of a poet-spider called Alberto Caeiro. He said:

The essential is to know how to see…
But this…
This calls for deep study,
Learning how to unlearn…

I try to get rid of what I learned,
I try to forget the way I was taught to remember,
And to scrape off the paint they used to cover my senses.

That reminds me of my friend scraping the paint off the walls of a one hundred year old house that he bought. Many were the layers, each resident painting a new color over the previous one. But he loved the house like a lover. He didn't want to put a on new dress over an old one. He wanted to see it naked. That meant a long *striptease,* successive scrapings, until it finally revealed its original nudity: ivory pine with sinuous brown stripes.

That's us. Houses. They keep painting us all our life long until there is no memory of our original body. Our face? It's lost. A mask of words. Who are we? We don't know. For us to know we need to forget, we need to unlearn.

Second spider, second web, Bernardo Soares: we only see what we are. Naively, we think that our eyes are pure, trustworthy, that they see things as they really are. What a mistake. Eyes are painters: they paint the external world with colors that live inside them. A luminous eye sees a colorful world; the eye of darkness sees a lightless world.

Not even God escaped. Being a mystery that nobody ever saw, God forbade humans, in the second commandment, even to try to make any painting of God: «You shall not make for yourself an image». They were threatened with the death penalty if they so much as pronounced God's name. But the humans disobeyed. They rushed to paint the great mystery the same way one paints a house. The more layers of paint they rolled on it, the more the mystery looked like the faces of the painters. Until the mystery disappeared, vanished, and was forgotten, buried under a mountain of words that humans piled up over the emptiness. Each one of them painted God in his or her own way.

Angelus Silesius says: The eye through which God sees me is the same eye through which I see God. Thus God became an avenger who operates a hell, an enemy of life who ordains death, a eunuch who ordains abstinence, a judge who condemns, an executioner who kills, a banker who collects debts, an inquisitor who ignites fires, a warrior who kills enemies—all exactly as the painters painted God.

And here we are before this ancient and gigantic mural where faces were painted, faces that the religious say are the faces of God. O my goodness! Mercy me! God cannot be so ugly. God has to be beautiful. Ugliness is the evil one, the demon, the Devil. Pictures of the ones who paint them, that's what these pictures are. The likeness is even less than in caricature. Caricature denotes some similarity. But here we have masks and idols. To return to God one has to undergo a great deal of forgetting. One has to unlearn what was learned. One has to scrape the paint.

Those who had not lost the memory of the mystery were horrified by that human audacity. They denounced it. One of them shouted that God was dead. Of course. He could not find God in that house of horrors. He proclaimed that we are God's murderers. He was accused of atheism. Yet, what he really wanted was to destroy all those masks and be able again to behold the infinite mystery.

Another person who did this was Jesus. «You have heard what was said to the ancients… But I say to you…» The God painted on the walls of the temple didn't reflect the God that Jesus saw. The God he talked about was appalling to the good people who defended good habits. He said that prostitutes would enter the Kingdom before religious folks. He said that the pious were like whitewashed tombs: externally clean, but internally stinking. He said that love was worthier than the law. He said that children were more divine than grownups. He said that God does not need sacred places —that every human being is an altar, no matter where he or she is.

He said this in a tender way. He told stories. To one of the stories the wall painters gave the name «Parable of the Prodigal Son». It is the story of a father and two sons. The older one was a nice, regular, dutiful and hardworking fellow. The younger one, a spendthrift and irresponsible rascal, gathered the portion of the inheritance that belonged to him. He went out into the world and spent everything on depravity and pleasure seeking. Then, hungry and out of money, he took a job as a pig herder. And then he remembered his life in his father's house, where the laborers had a better life than he now had. He imagined that his father might accept him back as a laborer, since he didn't deserve any longer to be treated as a son. He returned. The father saw him coming, and ran to meet him and hug him, and immediately ordered that a big party with barbecue and music be prepared for the occasion.

For the wall painters the story could have ended here. What a good story for calling sinners to repent. God always forgives. Not so fast! Still to come is the reaction of the older brother. Upon arriving from his labor, the older brother heard the music, smelled the barbecue, and was informed of what was going on. Resentful, and with good reason, he went into a rage against his father. The father made no distinction between creditor and debtor. If the father were like a confessor, his spendthrift son would have had to undergo some form of penance, to say the least.

The parable ends with an undecided argument between the father and the righteous son. But the argument is resolved once we understand their conversation. The younger son said: «Dad, you advanced to me my portion of the inheritance, and I spent it all. I am the debtor. You are the creditor». The father responded: «Son, I don't add up debts». The older son said: «Dad, I have been working hard without ever receiving a wage or vacation, and you never gave me a goat for a party with my friends. I am the creditor, and you are the debtor». The father answered: «Son, I don't add up credits».

The two sons were like each other and like all of us: they added up debts and credits. The father was different. Jesus paints a face of God that human wisdom cannot understand. God is not in the business of accounting. God doesn't add up either virtue or sins. This is how love is. It has no why's. It is reasonless. Love for love's sake. No accounting of good or of evil. With such a God the universe becomes a mother's lap. And fears vanish. The right name for the parable: «A father who doesn't know how to add». Or: «A father who has no memory».

The child God

The first to perceive it are the poets. This is so because their eyes are different. Because of that they see things in reverse. Poetry is things seen contrariwise. It's not a question of thinking, but a question of vision. When, after listening to a poem, people say that they did not understand it and ask for an explanation, it's because they have placed the poem in the wrong place, a place inhabited by thoughts. But a poem is not to be thought out in the head. It is rather to be seen by the eyes.

Poets, because their eyes are different, also see differently. They see the world contrariwise. Their truth is the opposite of the truth of grownups. Grownups think like this: children know nothing, the ones who know everything are the grownups; that being the case, children learn and grownups teach; childhood is the starting point; being grownup is the destination, the point of arrival.

Grownups want to surge ahead, to progress, to evolve. Poets know that the soul doesn't want to move ahead. The soul is moved by *saudade*. *Saudade* doesn't like to go ahead. It likes to go back.

Moving ahead may well be an ambiguity. According to an aphorism by T.S. Eliot: «In a world of fugitives the person taking the opposite direction will appear to run away…» Sometimes moving ahead means going farther and farther away. Grownups move forward. Poets appear to move backward, and the grownups say that they are running away. But that is not the case. Like the salmons, who leave the sea and return to the crystal clear waters where they were born, the poets want to return, as well, to their origins. There is where they find the truth that the grownups forgot. They run away from the madness of grownup life. They try to reencounter the simplicity of their childhood. I believe this is what Eliot had in mind when he wrote: «…And the end of all our exploring / Will be to arrive where we started / And know the place for the first time».

«My God, give me the age of five years old, give me your hand, and cure me of being a grownup…» The Brazilian poet Adélia Prado is sick. Sick with being grown up. To be grown up is to be sick. And the disease needs to be treated. If not treated it becomes insanity. To cure «adultitis» one must drink the tea of childhood and become a child again.

For this it would be good to read the poetry of the Brazilian poet Manoel de Barros. Manoel de Barros is a child. Whoever reads what he writes becomes a child. He plays with words.

> What I really wanted
> was to make toys with words.
> To make useless things…
> I wanted to advance to the starting point.
> Arriving where words become childlike.

Searching for the place where one started. The poetry of Manoel de Barros moves backward, far away from the madness of the grownup world. For that he does not spare words. And I arrange them the way I please:

I need to confound the meaningfulness. Purposelessness is healthier than solemnity. To clean the words of all solemnity —I use filth. I was born to deal with the useless, the futile, the good for nothing. I prefer machines that are good for not functioning: when they are full of sand, ants and moss —they may end up, miraculously, producing flowers. By the same miracle, abandoned latrines that are good for housing crickets may end up producing violets. Lord, I have the pride of worthlessness.

A man like this is a danger in any gathering of serious and responsible grownups.

The poet Bernardo Soares is explicit: grownups are stupid, children are smart.

Yes, sometimes, considering the hideous difference between the intelligence of children and the stupidity of grownups, I conclude that during our childhood we are protected by a guardian spirit that grants us its own astral intelligence; but which in due time, sorrowfully but moved by a higher law, abandons us as wild animal mothers abandon their more developed cubs.

I disagree only on one point: the astral intelligence does not abandon us because it is moved by a higher law. It abandons us because it is incompatible with adulthood. Grownup intelligence is heavy. It makes one sink. Childhood intelligence is light. It produces levitation.

Ricardo Reis, in his turn, says in a wisdom poem that the secret is for us to become disciples of children.

Lord, placid are
All the hours
That we waste,
If we waste them
As we place flowers
In a vase.
There is neither sadness

Nor joy
In our life.
Thus may we,
Careless sages, learn
Not to live life,
But to go through it,
Tranquil, placid,
Having the children
As our teachers
And our eyes full
Of nature…

When grownups teach we become scientists: we learn the science of dominating the world. When children teach we become wise: we learn the art of living.

Alberto Caeiro wrote a delightful poem about the Boy Jesus. He says that the Boy Jesus got tired of heaven and ran away to live with him, as a child like all the other children.

In heaven everything was false, and in conflict
With flowers, trees and stones.
In heaven, one must always be serious.
…He fled to the sun
And climbed down the first ray he caught.
Now he lives with me, in my village.
A child with a beautiful smile, and natural…

He taught me everything.
He taught me to look at things.
He points out to me all one can find in flowers.
He shows me how funny stones are
When we hold them in our hand
And slowly look at them…

The New Child who lives where I live
Stretches out one hand to me

And the other to all that exists,
And thus the three of us follow whatever road is there,
Jumping, singing and laughing,
Enjoying our common secret,
The knowledge that there is no mystery
Anywhere in the world
And that everything is worthwhile.

The Eternal Child always accompanies me.
My gaze follows where his finger points..
My hearing is joyfully attentive, and all sounds
Are his playful tickles in my ears.

…Afterwards he sleeps and I lay him down.
In my arms I carry him inside
And lay him down, undressing him slowly,
As if following a very clean
and purely motherly ritual, until he is nude.

He sleeps inside my soul
And sometimes wakes up during the night
And plays with my dreams.
He turns some of them upside down,
And places some of them over others
And alone he claps his hands,
Smiling at my sleeping.

When it is my time to die, little child,
May I become an even smaller child.
Take me in your lap
And carry me inside.
Undress my tired and human self
And lay me down on your own bed.
And, if I wake up, tell me stories
To make me sleep again.
And give me your dreams to play with

Until the dawn of that day
The day you know.

Christmas is a poem. In this poem God is revealed as a child. The grownup God is awful: grave, serious, never laughing, never sleeping, with eyes lacking eyebrows and always open, never forgetting anything, and making a list of everything in the accounting book that will be opened at the last judgment. The grownup God generates fear. There is no love in this God. This God has nothing in common with a child: a child is forgetful, laughing, playful, an eternal beginning. It is not for nothing that the Child Jesus runs away from the grownup God.

I prefer the child God. In the lap of the child God, I can sleep peacefully.

4

The stained glass window

I confess my lack of piety: I am unable to love God. I am unable to love anything in the abstract. I need a face, a voice, the gaze of an eye, the touch of a hand. I don't know what God is like. For this reason I am unable to love God. My master Alberto Caeiro's situation is even worse than mine, for he dares to affirm that he is unable even to think about God.

> To think about God is to disobey God,
> For God didn't want us to know God,
> That's why God didn't appear to us…

Love is the best tonic for memory. When the name of the loved thing is pronounced, it soon rises up from the dead and appears alive, in our imagination. And one's body is filled with *saudades. Saudade* is the symptom of the coming of a beloved and lost thing from the tomb. But the name of God does nothing to my memory. It doesn't provoke any resurrection. It doesn't make me feel *saudade* for anything. No response in my body.

I like the Bertolt Brecht poem, «Pleasures». It has no rhymes or rhythm. It is a simple list of some of the things that made him happy. Colored shards in a stained glass window.

The first morning's glance through the window.
The old book, once again found.
Faces filled with enthusiasm.
Snow, the change of seasons.
The newspaper.
The dog.
Taking a bath.
Swimming.
Old music.
Comfortable shoes.
Perceiving.
New music.
Writing, planting.
Traveling.
Singing.
Being a friend.

My «Pleasures» would be similar.

Waking up in the morning.
A hot shower.
Bach.
The good smell of coffee.
The sun just risen.
Walking,
eyes taking in the trees, the rain-wet grass,
the birds.
Thoughts that come to me while walking.
Planning my Zen garden.
Music.
Playing with my granddaughters.
Memories.

Books.

Calvin.

It's enough to write your «Pleasures». It is easy to be a poet when one's eyes are attentive to small joys.

Hermann Hesse wrote a book entitled *The Glass Bead Game* (*Das Glasperlenspiel*). It is the story of a monastic order whose members, instead of wasting their time in liturgical prayers and devotional rituals, occupied themselves in playing a game of glass beads. They knew that the gods prefer beauty to monotonous and senseless repetitions. The book doesn't describe the details of the game. But I know what it meant. As I write this page, I'm listening to Beethoven's Sonata number 27, opus 90. It is beautiful. Beethoven's colored beads, in this sonata, are the piano's notes.

Stained glass windows are games with colored glass beads, as well. It was in the poetry of a poet, a friend and former student of mine, Maria Antônia de Oliveira, that, for the first time, I saw life as a stained glass window.

Life is portrayed in time
forming a stained glass window,
an always incomplete figure,
of several colors,
shining when crossed by the sun.
Stones thrown at random,
irreversible.
Shattered fragments
Give way to holes.
Shards get lost
Over there.
Sometimes I find
The shards of life
That were mine,
That were alive.
Attentive, I examine them, trying to remember

what they used to be part of.

I have already found a little yellow shard

that, pretending, rose again,

an old friend.

I found another, a pointed and blue one, that brought on clouds

a kiss from the past.

There was a red shard

that made me cry abundantly,

without my figuring out

where it used to belong in me.

These stained glass windows, these colored glass beads —my body and soul love these, for ever. Love does not conform to the verdict of time— the shards of crystal losing themselves in the sea, the colored glass beads forever sinking in the river of time.

I wish that all I loved and lost would be returned to me. All these things housed in the immense colorful hole of my soul, that is called *saudade*.

For this I need God. I need God to cure me of *saudade*. It is said that the medicine is found in forgetting. But that is the last thing the one who loves desires. I heard of a man who was deeply in love with a woman taken away by death. In desperation, he appealed to the gods, asking them to use their power to send the woman back to him. With compassion, they told him that they could not bring back his beloved. They had no power over death. However, they could heal his suffering by making him forget her. To that he replied: «Anything but this. For my suffering is the only power that keeps her alive, by my side!»

Neither do I want the gods healing me by making me forget. I would rather have them give me back my glass beads. This is how I imagine God: as a thin and invisible nylon thread that searches for my glass beads at the bottom of the river and brings them back to me as a necklace. Not God's self (about whom I know nothing), but what God does with my beads.

I want a God like an artist, who gathers the shards of my stained glass, smashed by random stoning, and places them again in the cathedral's window so that the sun's rays may shine through them again.

What I want is a God who plays the glass bead game, in which I am one of them. One of the colorful glass beads of God's game.

5

Dear God, cure me of being a grownup!

The sky was dark. Disheveled grey clouds were blowing in the wind. No moon and no stars. As my mother used to say, on rainy days they hide so they won't get wet. It made one think of Prometheus—the one who stole fire from the gods—pitying the mortals for nights such as that. If it hadn't been for him, there would have been no fire crackling in the wood stove. The fire made all the difference. Outdoors it was cold, dark and sad. The kitchen was warm, glowing and cozy. On the stove the soup was boiling; its smell, mixed with the scent of smoke, was pleasant. There is no meal like soup. If I had to choose one meal to feed me for the rest of my life, it wouldn't be shrimp, beef or lasagna. It would be soup. Soup is the food of the poor, and can be made of leftovers. Thanks to the magic of fire, pan and water, any leftover can become good soup. There is even a story about stone soup.

Fire is the sorcerer's power. It has the power to make the real unreal. The eyes become charmed by the dance of the flames, the surrounding objects begin to lose their edges and are transformed into smoke. When this happens, those things that our memory has eternalized begin welling up from our forgetfulness, where they were kept. Fire makes us forget so that we can remember later. I always say to my patients that, instead of using a sofa, which reminds one of a doctor's examination table, I would prefer to be sitting with them by a lively fireplace. It is by the fire that the best kind of poetry comes to life. No wonder Pablo Neruda used to say that the substance of poets is fire and smoke.

«A long time ago I used to request of God a tradeoff: one year of life for one single day of my childhood. I don't do that anymore. I'm afraid he will accept the deal. I don't think it is prudent to dispose, like that, of my future years, since I don't know how many are there waiting for me». Thus spoke Maria Alice, with a soft voice and pure *saudade*. Wood stoves are themselves ghosts of a bygone world.

«When I was a child, in Mossâmedes, on cold nights we gathered in the kitchen, sitting around a basin full of live coals, placing our cold feet on the rungs of the chairs, enjoying the warmth of the fire».

«Mama would put a piece of cloth on her head and say: "I'm going to the back yard to get orange leaves to make us some tea", and she would proceed to lift the latch of the kitchen door. Every night, Papa would repeat the same warning: "My dear, you are going to catch a cold. It's dangerous to go out in the cold after being warmed up so by the fire". Mama wouldn't listen to him. And then, with those cups full of tea in our hands (oh how pleasant the scent of orange leaves was! I can still smell it now!), we asked Papa to tell us stories. He complied. They were always the same ones we had heard before. But it was as if he were telling them for the first time. They always brought on fear, thrills, and a shiver up and down our spines».

At that point Maria Alice began to wander. She remembered an uncle.

«In those days people were different. This uncle of mine had in his house a big front living room that was always empty and never used. Some folks wanted to rent it. He could get good money for that. He refused, and explained: "It's not for rent. It's from this room that I see the approaching rain way over there. If someone rented this, I would be sad when the rain arrived". Well, people were different then».

There was a silence. Then her poetic memory transformed itself into theological imagination.

«I believe that there are many heavens, one for each person. My heaven is not like yours. That's because heaven is the place where we meet the things that we loved and that time took away from us. The heavens keep all that memory loved».

I have already suggested that theology must be made in the kitchen. Clearly, not in just any kitchen. It doesn't work in a kitchen with either a gas or a microwave stove. I do understand that they are more functional. A woodburning stove is a complicated thing. It takes lot of art to light it. It demands care to keep the fire going. But what kind of dreams can a microwave oven bring me?

As Maria Alice talked, I returned in my mind to my childhood house, in the state of Minas Gerais. It was an old house with a rustic ceiling, a wooden floor with old, wide boards, and a leaking roof. That didn't bother us. We found it quite normal. A leakproof roof was unimagined. And it was good to hear the sound of raindrops falling in the basins and pots placed all over the house. It was the same on cold nights, with two differences. We turned off the lights. Not so much to save money as to make the magic stronger. In the dark, our faces reflected the light of the live coals, which made them reddish against the blackness. The imagination became tipsy, and the stories became scarier. The other difference was that there was always the steam locomotive's husky whistle. The train came by puffing, whistling around the curves, a husky, sad lamentation. It charred an old tree with jets of thousands of sparks, an incandescent ejaculation, and in my imagination that was exactly how the stars were born —they were sparks from a steam locomotive whose operator was God.

Fernando Pessoa used to be taken by metaphysical raptures at the sight of stone quays and departing ships. I feel the same way when I think about the steam locomotive and its husky whistle, which is not heard any more.

> The steam locomotive is a mechanical thing,
> but it crosses the night, the dawn, the day,
> it crossed my life,
> and became just feeling.

Thus was the husky lamentation of Adélia Prado, a poem of the whistling steam engine.

I remember my astonishment at my father's sixtieth birthday. I was so young! And he looked so old to me! Certainly he was already rowing his boat across the Deep River… The Deep River is the river of *saudades*. «Every *saudade* is a kind of old age», says Riobaldo. On September 15 I will be rowing deeper in the Deep River. The candle is getting shorter. And I join Maria Alice in a prayer: «Dear God, give me the age of five years old, and cure me of being a grownup».

Part Two

Gestures and Words

1

The Baptized One

My son Sergio came to me with a strange request. He asked me to prepare a ritual for the baptism of my granddaughter Mariana. I told him that to come up with a ritual one needs to believe. And I don't believe. For many years now the words of priests and preachers have sounded empty to me, although I continue to be fascinated by the beauty of Christian symbols, when they are beheld in silence.

He didn't give up. He insisted: «But you performed my wedding!» Yes, it's true! I remember how he instructed me on that ritual: «Dad, don't use words of religion. Use words of poetry!» And that was what I did. I used passages from the Song of Songs, an erotic biblical poem that makes the sanctimonious blush: «Your two breasts are like two fawns, twins of a gazelle!» «Your lips distill nectar… honey and milk are under your tongue…» (Song of Solomon 4:5,11) I amuse myself thinking of the faces of popes and bishops when they read these texts. These passages were followed by verses from the Brazilian poets Drummond, Vinícius and Adélia —and the ceremony concluded not with the annoying and overused wedding march of Wagner or Mendelssohn, but with the *Valsinha* (little waltz) of the popular Brazilian composer Chico Buarque de Holanda, while all the guests, young and old, found their partners and danced. It was beautiful, and beauty enhances believing.

Then I remembered a passage in Alex Haley's book, *Roots* —about an African tribal naming ritual.

Omoro, the father, stood by the side of his wife, facing the villagers. Then, while everyone watched, he lifted up the baby boy three times, whispering each time, in his ear, the name he had chosen for him. It was the first time that the name was being pronounced. The villagers knew that each human being should be the first to learn who he or she is. Drums were heard. Omoro whispered the same name in his wife's ear, and she smiled with pleasure. Then it was time for the whole village to hear it: «The name of the first born son of Omoro and Binta Kinte is Kunta!» After the conclusion of the ritual, Omoro, alone, carried his little son to the end of the village, and there he lifted him up to heaven and softly said: «Fend killing dorong leh warrata ke iteh ted» [Behold the only thing bigger than you!].

That ritual inspired me and I decided to come up with one for the occasion, since I didn't know any that pleased me.

I rearranged the living room. I pushed the coffee table towards the fireplace. By the head of the table I placed a very old little bench —on which Mariana would be sitting— and, on each side a chair, one for the father and other for the mother. At the foot of the table I placed a big candle. It was Mariana's candle —the one that will accompany her during her whole life and be lighted on all her birthdays. On each side of her candle, I placed a long colored candle. Then I placed candles of all kinds and colors all over the room. Also on the table, near Mariana, I placed a wooden plate with a bunch of grapes.

Once the guests were gathered, the ritual started. I spoke: «Mariana, we are here to tell you the story of your name. Everything began with a great darkness». All the lights were then turned out, and we all could hear, in the background, the sound of a flute played by Jean-Pierre Rampal.

«This is how it was in the belly of your mother, a dark, tranquil and silent place. There you lived for nine months. Then you got tired of it and said: "I want light!" Your mother heard your request and gave you what you wanted. She gave you to the light. She gave birth. You were born».

Mariana's mother and father then lighted the big candle which shone, alone, in the middle of the room.

«See what happened! Your light filled the room with joy. All the faces are smiling at you. And moved by this joy, all the guests will light their own candles».

Then the godfather and the godmother lighted the long colored candles, followed by the rest of the guests who lighted the ones they had picked up from some place in the room.

Earlier, as the guests were arriving, I had handed little cards to them, on which they were to write a good wish for Mariana. After all the candles were lighted, I said:

«You brought so much joy to us that each one of us wrote, on a little card, a good wish for you. Now take this little basket and go from guest to guest collecting what they wrote. You are going to keep these cards for life».

And there went Mariana, with her little basket, her great blue eyes, from person to person, being blessed by all.

«Everyone has given you a good thing», I said, after she had collected the cards. «Now is the time for you to give a good thing to everyone, as well. You are little, round and sweet as a grape. That's what explains this bunch of grapes near you. This is what you are going to do: your godparents will make a little chair with their crossed arms, and sitting in that chair you will give a grape, a kind of piece of yourself, to each person in the room».

So it was that, slowly, Mariana celebrated, unaware, this unusual Eucharist: «This sweet and round grape is my body».

After the Eucharist, I said to Mariana:

«Now, in conclusion, each one of us is going to say your name. Pay attention. Your name is just one name. But each one of us will say it in a different musical tune. That is because you are loved in many different ways».

And so it happened that, lighted by the candles, each one of us, looking into the girl's eyes, said: «Mariana», «Mariana», «Mariana», «Mariana»…

Those who looked into Mariana's eyes could see that, as she heard her name repeated, her eyes were filling with tears.

2

Prayer

Today I am going to write about the art of praying. You may say that this is not a topic that a psychotherapist should deal with. Intercession and prayer is the concern of priests and preachers, to be dealt with in churches, monasteries and cults. I happen to know that what people want, when they go to a therapist, is to learn how to pray. Of course they are not aware of this. They talk about thousands of other things. They don't know that the soul desires just one thing, whose name we have forgotten. As T.S. Eliot said, we have

> …knowledge of motion, but not of stillness…
> Knowledge of words, and ignorance of the Word.
> All our knowledge brings us nearer to our ignorance,
> All our ignorance brings us nearer to death…

Therapy is the search for this forgotten name. And once we have remembered and pronounced it, with all the passion of body and soul, we give to this act the name of poetry. We could also call it prayer.

Behind our loquacity (we talk too much and listen too little) lies hidden the desire to pray. Many words are said, because we have not yet found the only words that matter. I would like to demonstrate this —and the demonstration begins with a walk. As we begin, open your eyes as widely as possible. See how this world is so bright and beautiful! So much so, that Nietzsche even composed a poem about it:

> …my dream looked upon this finite world…as if a round apple offered itself to my hand, a ripe, golden apple with cool, soft, velvet skin… as if tender hands brought me a shrine, a shrine open for the delight of shy, adoring eyes, thus the world offered itself to me today…

Everything is okay. Everything is in order. Nothing prevents the delight of this gift. No one is ill. There is no terrible financial deprivation. One even likes the people one lives with, without which life would have a sour taste.

But this is not all. Besides the satisfaction of basic and vital needs, the soul longs for beauty. And beauty the world has in abundance. It can be found everywhere, in the moon, in the street, in the constellations, in the seasons, in the sea, in the air, in the rivers, in the waterfalls, in the rain, in the scent of vegetation, in the twinkling light on the wrinkled waters of the lagoon, in the gardens, in faces, in voices and gestures.

Besides beauty, there are pleasures that dwell in the eyes, ears, nose, mouth and skin. As on the last day of creation, we have to agree with the Creator: looking at what had been created, the Creator saw that it was very good.

Yet, without any explanation, and in spite of all these things, the soul remains empty. The poet Álvaro Campos put this feeling in a poem:

Give me lilies, lilies
And also roses.
…Chrysanthemums, dahlias,
Violets, and sunflowers
Above all the flowers.

…But no matter how many roses and lilies you give me,
I'll never feel that life is enough.
I'll still be missing something…

My pain is as useless
As a bird cage in a birdless land,
And my pain is as silent and sad
As a stretch of beach untouched by the sea.

As if a gray cloud of sadness and boredom covered everything. Life is heavy. Walking is difficult, dragging one's body. People come to the therapist pretending that they are missing a lily here, a rose there, a chrysanthemum somewhere. They are looking, in all this, for the only thing that really matters: joy. But it so happens that the sources of joy cannot be found in the outer world. It is useless to be given all the flowers in the world. The sources of joy are to be found in the inner world.

The inner world: religious people call it the soul. What is the soul? The soul is the landscape that exists inside our bodies. Our body is a frontier between the outer and inner landscapes. And they are different. «We have two eyes», said Angelus Silesius, a medieval mystic. «With one, we see the things that happen in time. With the other, we see what is eternal and divine». In a certain hidden spot in the soul's landscape lie the sources of joy —the lost sources. Once lost, the soul's landscape fades away and the body feels like an empty house. And when the house is empty, joy disappears. And the outer landscape becomes ugly (in spite of being beautiful).

The external world is a world where caged birds are bought and sold. There are those who think that if they buy the right bird, they will have joy. But caged birds, no matter how beautiful, cannot offer joy. There are no cages in the soul.

Joy is a bird that comes in only when it wants. It is free. The best we can do is to break all the bird cages, and to sing a love song in the hope that the bird will hear us. Prayer is the name given to the song that invokes joy.

Many prayers are the result of senselessness. There are those who think the universe would be better if God followed their advice. They ask God to give them caged birds, many birds. In this way, Protestants and Catholics are alike. They prattle. They don't even try to listen. They don't realize that prayer is a lamentation, a «sigh of the oppressed creature». Can there be a more beautiful definition? These are the words of Karl Marx. Sigh: a lamentation without words, a longing to hear divine music, music that, if heard, would bring us joy.

I like to read prayers. Prayers and poems are the same thing: words proceeding from silence, asking the silence to speak to us. According to Ricardo Reis, it is in silence, in the space between words, that one can hear the voice of «whatever Being, alien to us», who speaks to us. The Being's name? It doesn't matter. All names are metaphors for the nameless Great Mystery that surrounds us. I like to read prayers because they say the words I wish I had said, but was unable to say. Prayers bring music into my silence.

Promises

I don't care what my enemies think of me. What they think reveals nothing about my person —but it says a lot about their digestive condition. Nietzsche used to say that there were those who didn't like him, because his words were fire in their mouths. But words, like hot pepper, can be fire in one's mouth. Therefore, I don't care if someone doesn't think well of me.

However, if my friends don't think well of me —that will make me suffer. If they, being my friends, think evil of me, this means that there is a bit of truth in their thoughts. My friends' thoughts are a kind of mirror. I will be ashamed and begin to avoid being with them.

God is like people. God doesn't care at all what the Devil and his gang think about God. But it is a wholly different matter when the slander and wickedness come precisely from those —surprise!— who think they are God's friends. I even believe that this is the meaning of the Church's doctrine that the Son of God continues to be sacrificed every day —as many times as the ritual of the Mass is performed. I always wondered if these sacrifices would ever end. Only late in life did I understand that the reason Our Lord Jesus Christ never ceases to be crucified is because those who say that they are Christ's sons, friends, worshipers and devotees never cease to spread lies, all over the world, about Christ's character and sufferings. They don't have the courage to do so openly. Openly, they show only piety and fear. They say «thanks be to God», «if God so pleases», «praise be to God»; they make the sign of the cross, go to church, light candles, read the Bible. But, secretly, with closed mouths, without words, they spread the idea that God is an abnormal, sadistic, and corrupt being, and cheap. This is the worst cross to bear: the disfavor of friends. If I had friends like that, I would find a way to move far away from them.

If you do not understand what I'm saying, I'll explain.

When we give something, we are saying what we think about the person who is receiving the present. I give water to a plant, because I know that plants like water. I give a dog a bone, because I know that dogs like bones. I give seeds to a bird, because I know that birds like seeds.

The same is true of presents to people. I went to a gift shop with two friends, a married couple. There were many choices. Among others, some beautiful colored aprons. The wife whispered softly in my ear, teasingly: «If he [her husband] buys me an apron I'll divorce him». Of course. The present would be saying: «Darling, you look so beautiful in the kitchen!» But she didn't want to be defined as a cook. A present says what we think the other is.

A CD of classical music says that the other, exactly as he or she exists in my head, is a lover of fine music. If it is a CD of a jazz saxophone, the image of the other will be different, more sensual. A poetry book will say to the other that he or she is seen as a sensitive person and a lover of silence. Pots, tools, toys, scarves, men's silk shorts, lace-trimmed brassieres, an erotic art book, a bottle of wine, Bibles and rosaries, a box of chocolate: each one of these presents says to the receiver what I think of him or her.

God deserves presents as well. God wants to be happy too. Those who say that they like God are inspired to bring presents to God, as the Magi did: the best of all, those that give pleasure. Presents to make God laugh with happiness, presents to make God turn again into a child! The present that I give must make the desires of the other come true. And what are God's desires —judging by the presents offered to God?

A long time ago, the most fervent devotees performed self-flagellation with whips and sharp pointed knives. When I was a child, I used to see women in religious processions carrying heavy stones on their heads, as a present to God. Nowadays this type of present is considered outmoded. God improved and now accepts only the scabs of more delicate wounds. In the store of presents to God one can find, for example, the following options: to walk, on your knees, the trail to Father Cícero's chapel; to climb up, on your knees, the stairway of *Igreja da Penha* (Church of the Rock); to drag a cross, on foot, for forty miles; to fast for three days; to abstain from beer for a whole month; to refrain from drinking coca-cola for nine months; to abstain from any kind of sexual activity until grace is granted.

What do these presents say about God's character? They say that God is not God, that God is a monstrous and sadistic being who feels happy when we suffer, a corrupt being who exchanges grace for pain. If I were God, I would find a way to move far away, to another universe inhabited only by plants and animals. Plants and animals understand God better than we do.

Therefore, while asking to be forgiven for so many offenses, I suggest that at the passing of the year we bring beautiful resolutions to God, resolutions that show that we consider God to be as normal and beautiful as we are. God is not sadistic. God doesn't have an orgasm when we suffer. God suffers when we suffer and laughs when we laugh. Thus, if we offer presents of happiness, God will be happy and will come back.

I will take a walk every day, without worrying about exercise, in some woods or garden of this marvelous universe, for sheer pleasure. I will purchase a cocker spaniel puppy. I will spend time watching the flight of the birds, the shape of the clouds, the leaves of the trees. I'm going to watch *Il Postino* again. I'm going to run away from agitation, noise and confusion. I'll cultivate solitude and silence: a sacred space. I'll plant a Zen garden with water and wind chimes. I'm going to listen to lots of music, Gregorian chants, Bach, Beethoven, Mahler, César Frank. I'm going to read the complete works of Fernando Pessoa. I'm going to learn to cook. I'm going to receive my friends. I'm going to drink beer, wine, Jack Daniels. I'm going to play with things and with people.

So help me God. And may God be pleased with my resolutions.

What I love in the Church

I believe the Pope should promulgate an encyclical making obligatory the use of Latin in the Church. That would convert me. Modern priests, who like to teach and to raise political consciousness, will say that nobody understands Latin. To that I reply: but that is the only way to convert me. It would be necessary for me not to understand anything. The charismatics are right. They speak in unknown tongues, and in that unknowingness they meet their God. A God who is comprehended cannot be that great. A sea that is comprehended is nothing but an aquarium. A. Gottlieb said that his favorite symbols were those that he didn't understand. I say Amen to that. That's why I love Latin: because I don't understand it. The same way I don't understand the creeks, the birds, the wind, my grandchildren, and love them all.

Mine was a Protestant education. The Protestants disliked the Catholics. And not without reason. Latin was a priest's thing. Therefore the Protestants didn't study Latin, and I didn't learn it. But I love Latin because of its music. Pure crystal. Beauty of the cosmic spheres. If popes, bishops and priests spoke only Latin, I would become a convert to the Church precisely to not understand the lyrics of their singing, and to hear the melody and soft charm of their chant.

I have a theory about the Pentecost. As is well known, one day the apostles spoke in a language that they knew, and the people around them heard it as if it were their own, although they were foreign tourists and their languages were those of the countries they came from. I believe there is only one explanation for this miracle. The apostles didn't speak. They sang. It was the birth of the *vocalise*. *Vocalise* is a song without words. The voice is used as an instrument. Pure voice, pure music, pure beauty, without meaning, without saying anything. For that reason, because of saying nothing, everybody understands. Those who don't know what I am talking about should listen to the *Bachianas Brasileiras* number 5, of Villa Lobos, for soprano and eight cellos. Or Gabriel Fauré's *Pavane* sung by Barbara Streisand. Beauty doesn't need meaning. It saves without saying anything. Yes, I would be a convert to a religion in which words would be silenced so that the music could be heard.

Therefore, I stand before the Church, repeating Fernando Pessoa's poem:

Stop your singing!
Stop, because,
As I heard it,
I heard also
Another voice
Coming from the interstices
Of the gentle enchantment
Which with your singing
Came unto us.
I heard you
And I heard it
At the same time
And different

Singing together.
And the melody
Which was not there
If I well remember
Makes me cry.

I don't want to understand whatever is said. In truth, I don't want anything to be said. «The word», says Adélia, «is the masking of something more grave, something deaf-mute, something invented to be silenced».

At this moment I'm listening to a Gregorian chant of Schola Ungarica. Now come the feminine voices of the boys. They sing in Latin. What are they saying? I don't know. I don't want to know. Beauty is enough for me. Beauty makes love with the body. That's why the body trembles and cries. Words stay in the head. Which brings to my mind the saying of the Protestant philosopher Kierkegaard, who knew about these things: «Truth is not in *what* is said, but in *how* it is said». God is not in the lyrics. God is in the tune.

In order to love the Church, I stop thinking. I need to put my intellect to sleep. I recite the verse of Alberto Caeiro: «To think is to be sick in the eyes». Once thinking ceases, I am transformed into a being of the senses and only the senses, exactly as I was born. Then I am eye, ear, nose, mouth, skin. I see, I hear, I smell, I taste, I feel myself touched. I love the Church for her erotic mischiefs, for what she does to my senses.

The Gregorian chant continues. It proceeds in its task of sensual seduction. It tenderly penetrates my ears like a soft velvet snake, until it reaches the center of my soul, where my erogenous spots are found. Each sense has an erogenous spot of its own. I deliver myself to the melody. I'm defeated. Gregorian chant, probably the greatest musical production of the Catholic Church (as is well known, J.S. Bach was Protestant), makes me forget all that theologians, bishops and popes have said in all the centuries of the life (and death) of the Church.

The seduction of music does not stop there. I love bells. For me, one of the most beautiful verses in the Portuguese language comes from Álvaro de Campos: «Ah, the whole quay is a *saudade* made of stone!» I would add: «And every bell is a *saudade* made of bronze». Quays announce departures and distances. Bells announce worlds that no longer exist. There is nothing more contradictory than the sound of bells in big cities. To cities belong the sounds of honking, of electric rails, of loudspeakers. The music of the bell is a butterfly that enters into a prison cell. It speaks of worlds that exist only in *saudade*. Music comes to us from undefined places in a distant past. Just as I believe that God dwells in *saudade*, the peal of bells, which says nothing and means nothing, is an altar

made out of sounds. If I were the Pope I would rule that bells should be rung three times every day: at six in the morning, at noon, and at six in the evening. Bells, more than many sermons, would make the body remember God.

Where are the bells? I don't know. The Church has been modernized. I think it has become ashamed of old things. In the city of São Paulo there was a seminary, and in the center of its yard there was a bell that marked the rhythm of life. The bell has disappeared. In its place there is something modern, a strident device, similar to a clerical voice.

And what about the seduction of the eyes? The terrifying paintings of Grünenwald, the most horrifying crucified Christs that I ever saw, the nightmares of Bosch, the transparent Christs of Salvador Dalí, the Madonnas of Raphael, the *Pietà* of Michelangelo. Being afraid of idolatry, Protestantism never produced anything comparable to these masterpieces. Protestantism has always been afraid of the objective representation of beauty: it is easy for the charm of beauty to become a fetish. Thus, to avoid the risk of temptation, the Protestants followed the gospel's advice to the letter: they tore out their own eyes.

I stopped writing, for a while, to skim through a marvelous book I just bought: *Le vitrail* (the stained glass window). It's about the art of working with glass, colors, transparencies and light. O, how beautiful is a Gothic cathedral, when sunlight comes through the stained glass window. This cannot become an idol. This is like a rainbow: it cannot be touched.

I love stained glass windows. A wonderful poet, Maria Antonia, a professor in the state of Mato Grosso, taught me about them.

> Life is portrayed in time
> forming a stained glass window,
> an always incomplete figure,
> of several colors,
> shining when crossed by the sun.
> Stones thrown at random,
> irreversible.
> Shattered fragments
> Give way to holes.

I also love the empty spaces of Gothic cathedrals, where the soul flies. I love the monasteries and their cloisters, the gardens, the fountains, the vegetation. And the incense, the perfumed erotization of my body.

You may have understood: I love, in the Church, all that came from the hands of artists. However, when I hear the explanations of theologians and teachers, the charm breaks down, and I wish they were speaking in Latin so that I couldn't understand what they were saying. Lyrics put an end to the music. That being the case, all I want is to repeat the saying of Fernando Pessoa: «Stop your singing...» Let beauty, without words or catechisms, evangelize the world. God is Beauty.

Part Three

Fears

Hell

You ask me if I believe in the existence of Hell, a place where God incarcerates souls condemned to endless suffering, for eternity. I won't answer. I'll tell you a story, and you will come to your own conclusion.

Once upon a time there was an agreeable old man who lived in a house surrounded by gardens. The old man loved his garden and cared for it personally. Indeed it was he, himself, who planted it —all kinds of flowers, fruit trees of several species, fountains, waterfalls, lakes full of fish, ducks, geese, magpies. The birds loved his garden. They built their nests in its trees, and fed on its fruits. The butterflies and bees went from flower to flower, filling the space with their dances. So kind was the old man, that his garden was open to all: children, old people, sweethearts, tired grownups. All of them could have some fruit and swim in the crystal clear lakes. The old man's garden was a real paradise, a place of happiness.

The old man loved all creatures; there was always a tender smile on his face. If one paid a bit of attention, one could see that there were deep scars on his hands and legs. It is said that, on a certain day, he saw a child being attacked by a wild dog, and he fought the dog. That's how he got his scars.

At the end of the back yard behind the old man's house there was a mysterious woods that became a forest. It was a different kind of garden, because the woods, not touched by the old man's hands, grew wild, as is the case with all forests. To the old man, forests were as beautiful as gardens. When the sun set and night fell, the old man would do something that intrigued everybody: he took to the forest, and only returned at sunrise. Nobody knew what he did in the forest, and the rumor mills began to work. Humans have always had a tendency to imagine sinister things. In this case, the gossip was that when night came, the old man became a monstrous being, like a werewolf, and that there was a deep cave in the forest where the old man kept, chained, people he didn't like, and that he tortured them with sharp knives and red hot irons. Furthermore —so went the gossip— he delighted in their suffering.

There were others who disputed this. For them, there was neither a cave, nor prisoners, nor torture. That kind of thing existed only in the imagination of wicked people, the ones who came up with such rumors. What really happened was that the old man was a mystic who loved forests, and walked into their darkness for silence and communion with the mystery of the universe.

It is up to you to decide which version you will believe. Important: no one has ever penetrated the dark forest. All that is there are human fantasies. The fantasies of cruel and vengeful people. The fantasies of people moved by love.

If you decide to believe that the old man has a torture chamber that gives him pleasure, then you will have to believe, as well, that he is a monster who plays with children during the day and tortures defenseless people during the night. His daylight goodness is nothing but a farce. I could never love such an old man. Could you? Before an old man like this, one feels horror rather than love. Whoever believes that God has an eternal chamber for endless torturing, cannot love, but only fear God. However, since God is love, whatever is feared cannot be God. It can only be the Devil.

But if you believe that such a torture chamber is simply an invention of wicked hearts, then you will love the old man even more.

You understand that this story is a parable about God. Whoever believes in Hell really believes awful things about God. Therefore the crucial question, in this inquiry about the existence of Hell, is: what do you think about God? I imagine that the old man must have cried bitterly when he learned of the gossip that was circulating about him. I believe that God cries too, when religious people, who say they are God's servants, spread rumors that God delights in the sufferings of prisoners in God's torture chambers. If the old man were not so kind, I think such servants would be the ones that he would send for a short stay in Hell, if Hell existed.

On the salvation of my soul

Things I have said about God have caused many of my readers to be fearful for the future of my soul in the next world. They believe that I will go to Hell. In Hell there are sinners who stole, fornicated and killed, as well as those who dared to have their own ideas. To think right, for these readers, is to think the way priests and pastors think. To reassure them, I'll explain.

About the Bible. I have studied it a lot, and love it. For me it is a poem whose words comfort me and make me a wiser person. However, one needs to establish a distinction between the written words of the poem and what people think when they read them. Any act of reading is also interpretation, that is, the thinking of the readers. Every sermon is the thinking of a person, not God's thinking. The interpretation is different from the poem. Each church, each congregation, each sect organizes itself around a particular interpretation, the word of people. But each has the illusion that his or her interpretation is the Word of God. As the Word of God, it is the only true word. It is very pretentious to think that only my sect has the correct interpretation and all the others have it wrong. What I write is my interpretation, which is as problematic as any other. One shouldn't forget the wise affirmation of the apostle Paul: we don't know things directly; what we see are tremulous and obscure reflections, as in a poorly polished mirror. We should never confuse the reflection in the mirror with the true face, which no one ever saw. Of God, the only absolutely certain thing that we know is love (see 1 Cor. 13).

What is faith? It is also a question of interpretation. There are those who think that faith is a magical resource which assures us that God will listen to us. To them the God who doesn't listen to our requests is a weak God. They want guarantees. In my interpretation faith is a relationship between trust and God: it is to float in a sea of love, as we float in water. Who loves their parents more? Those who are faithful to their parents because they give them the presents they ask for, or those who love their parents even though they don't give them presents? Do we love our parents for the presents, the blessings, that they give us, or for themselves? I love God even if God doesn't give me any presents.

I believe that Christ fills all the spaces of the universe. Martin Luther used to talk about the ubiquity of the body of Christ, and said that Christ is present even in the smallest leaf, although his name is not written there. Whoever loves breathes Christ, even without mentioning his name. James says that the demons know everything about God, yet they are demons. The reformers used to talk about the *Christus absconditus,* that is, the hidden, invisible, nameless Christ in all creation. Christ is in anyone who loves, even if he or she doesn't quote the scriptures or doesn't know the name of Christ. Christ cannot be bottled up in religious names. That would negate his omnipresence, and that would be heresy.

The Holy Scriptures are a huge book. Many say that the whole book is inspired. If they really believe this, then all the texts must be an object of our love, since they are «words of God». But I notice that those who say this also behave as if some texts are more inspired than others. For instance, I have never heard a sermon, whether by a Catholic or a Protestant, about: «…my bride; honey and milk are under your tongue… your two breasts are like two fawns, twins of a gazelle…» (Song of Solomon 4: 11, 5); «Go, eat your bread with enjoyment, and drink your wine with a merry heart… Enjoy life with the wife whom you love, all the days of your vain life» (Ecclesiastes 9:7,9). Why the silence? I believe that, secretly, they think that some texts are more words of God than others.

As for the destiny of my soul, don't worry. Jesus himself told the pharisees, those religious people who were always quoting the Scriptures and trying to convert others, that the prostitutes would enter the kingdom of heaven before them. Important: Jesus didn't say «penitent prostitutes». The actual prostitutes enter ahead of them. Then, after the prostitutes, come the hypocrite pharisees and whatever else God created. God created everything, right? If God created everything, can you believe that God would deliver to the Devil all that came from God's hands? A God who is all love cannot have, in eternity, a chamber of endless tortures in which souls suffer for their bodily sins. Temporal debts become eternal debts? Only if God were the owner of a bank. The one who would be happy with this is the Devil. And do you believe that God would be at the service of the Devil's desires? In the end God's love triumphs! And all of us —you, I, the prostitutes, and everything— will be marching in.

Again, about Hell

God sent a terrible punishment to the soldiers of the Philistines for having stolen the most sacred thing that the chosen people had: the ark in which were kept the stones with the ten commandments chiseled on them. The terrible punishment was that all the soldiers had an attack of hemorrhoids. The text says that their suffering was so intense that their groaning could be heard from far away (I Samuel 5:12). If I were God, I would send a similar plague to all who spread gossip about God having special torture chambers for God's own delight, called Hell. I can't imagine anything more horrible that one could say against God, because it is unimaginable that a God of love would impose eternal punishments for sins that were committed in time. And these gossipers even justify their rumors by saying that God behaves like that because God is just. They don't take into account that divine justice is what God does to heal God's creation of all kinds of suffering. It is Jesus, himself, who says: «If you… who are evil, know how to give good gifts to your children, how much more will your Father in heaven give good things to those who ask him!» (Matthew 7:11).

My reasoning was not sufficient, and many accused me of heresy for not believing in what is found in the sacred texts. They argued: «Was it not Jesus, himself, who told the parable of the rich man and Lazarus after their deaths, the latter going to heaven and the former to Hell? If Jesus said so, one has to believe».

I do believe. I believe in parables as I believe in poems. Poems and parables are metaphors about the scenarios of the human soul. A psychoanalyst would say: «These are dreams that throw light into the dark basements of the unconscious». I remember a woman who told me that, in a dream, she had a tumor inside her head, just by the side of her ear, which throbbed and ached a lot. Suddenly the tumor began to leak out through the ear. And what came out of the ear —amazingly— was not pus, but seeds of passion fruit! I would be crazy if I interpreted the dream literally, and sent the woman to a neurosurgeon to extract the tumor. This dream was a story through which her unconscious revealed, in a gentle way and with a bit of humor, a suffering and a pleasure that she, consciously, refused to understand. Of course there was no tumor in her head. The tumor was in her soul, which was trying to expel passion fruit seeds! (This is not the time for me to explain what the passion fruit's seeds really meant).

And the story of king-poet David's seduction of Bathsheba, the wife of one of his generals, impregnating her. As a cover-up for his sin, he ordered the killing of Uriah, her husband. Nathan, the prophet, came to the king, and told him the following parable: «There were two men in a certain city, one rich and the other poor. The rich man had many flocks and herds; but the poor man had nothing but one little lamb, which he loved very much. But the rich man, wanting to have a barbecue, stole and slaughtered the only lamb of his poor neighbor». After he finished telling the parable, the prophet asked the king: «What kind of punishment does this man deserve?» David answered: «…the man who has done this deserves to die». And the prophet replied: «You are that man». The rich man, owner of one thousand lambs, never existed. Neither did the poor man who had just one lamb. The prophet spoke by means of metaphors. A parable does not have the purpose of providing verifiable information about the external world. Its true objective is to reveal the inner world.

The same can be said of the parables of Jesus. The prodigal son, the model son and the compassionate father never existed. Neither did the woman who lost the coin, nor the good Samaritan and the poor man who was clobbered by the thieves. These are stories that never happened. Never, because they always happen in our souls. Whoever believes that they actually happened in some place, in the past, does not realize that they speak about what is happening here and now.

If you are going to believe in the parables literally, then get ready! Jesus told a parable about a man who was about to get married to ten virgins in one single night (Mt 25:1-12). If this parable is to be interpreted in the same way as the one about the rich man and Lazarus, literally, then we will have to arrive at the conclusion that the kingdom of heaven is a macho place, where men marry ten women in one single night. And, if this is true of the kingdom of heaven, it must also be true of the earth, for it is said in the Lord's Prayer: «…on earth, as it is in heaven…»

The parable of the rich man and Lazarus doesn't refer to an external place called Hell. It refers to the never extinguishable fire, in the soul, called remorse. What the rich man wanted was for Lazarus «to dip the tip of his finger in water and cool my tongue». (Lk 16:24). He wanted to be forgiven. But Lazarus had already died. The rich man was condemned to suffer the pain of his remorse.

Petrus

Years ago I climbed a mountain. Beholding the valley which opened out far below, I began to wonder about the millennia. For how long had that mountain beheld the valley? Ten thousand years? One hundred thousand years? Then I saw a white stone, an unperturbed witness of the passage of time, and decided to bring it to my office. I'm looking at it just now. It hasn't changed in the least: the same pinkish white coloration, the same pattern of grooves, the same shape. It will remain like that indefinitely. Stones are alien to time. They are immutable because they are dead.

Along with the stone I also brought in some small plants. They didn't survive. They felt uneasy in my house. Plants can react to the environment. They like it or dislike it. They grow green or wither away. Stones don't feel anything. For them all things are the same. They are unconcerned about the surrounding world. They are always the same, because they are dead. But plants live. And because they do they are always transforming themselves into another thing. Life cannot stand sameness. To be born, to grow, to age and to reproduce. No plant is identical to itself in a subsequent moment in time. Stones aren't born, they don't grow and don't reproduce. They are eternal. They are always the same. Dead.

Life abhors sameness. A scientist friend of mine who specialized in bamboo lent me a wonderful book on the subject. I learned that bamboo blooms. I was surprised. I had never seen a flowering bamboo. I had thought that bamboo reproduces asexually, the mother plant bringing forth sprouts identical to itself. But the book said that each species of bamboo blooms approximately every hundred years, all over the world. After a sexual orgy of exchange of genes, of ejaculation of seeds, the bamboo plants die. New ones will be born from the seeds. They will not be the same as they were. Because the seed is precisely this: life refusing to be the same, life aware that in order to go on living it needs «to cease to be» so as «to become» another thing. If there is no mixing of genes, if the plant wants to stay always the same, it degenerates. It has to cease to be the same thing and has to transform itself into another. A piece of evangelical wisdom applies to the plants: «Those who want to save their life will lose it». Those who remain the same will die. Or will transform themselves into stone. In procreation there is always a little bit of death. «Die and transform yourself», said Goethe. «Only where there are tombs are there resurrections», said Nietzsche. «Unless a grain of wheat falls onto the earth and dies, it remains just a single grain; but if it dies, it bears much fruit», said Jesus.

«Empty shell. The cicada sang itself out». A haiku of Bacho if I am not mistaken. Before there was an empty shell, the cicada sang underground songs —life happened in the depth of the earth. But suddenly life became something else. The underground cicada began to dream dreams of open air and flight. It came out of the earth. Its shell was no longer able to contain the life which grew inside. It broke open. From it came another being, a winged being, an aerial being. We humans are like the cicada, except that our shells are made of words. As life grows, the verbal shells transform themselves into prisons. They have to be abandoned so that life may go on. «The snake that cannot shed its skin perishes. So do the spirits who are prevented from changing their opinions». A Nietzsche aphorism.

Ecumenism was a bamboo blooming: the wish to exchange ideas, the wish to become seed, to fall on the ground, to cease to be what one was and to become another thing. The possibility of «being born anew»: the old person becoming a child.

But now the Vatican reaffirms its stony immutability, its sameness, the eternity of its shell of words: «*Quod semper, ubique et ab omnibus creditum est*». The official Catholic theologians canonized Parmenides over Heraclitus. They reaffirmed the stone over the seed. Bamboo is forbidden to bloom. Why bloom? It's unnecessary. The Church possesses the truth. She does not need anyone else. The game of exchanging seeds is forbidden. Dialogue is only to convert others. Why listen when I possess the whole truth? Why allow others to speak, if what they say can only be a lie? All who pretend to possess the truth are doomed to be inquisitors. Thus, over all the seeds, the curse of silence.

In Pocinhos do Rio Verde, a little village in Southern Minas Gerais, there is a mountaintop of massive rock, named Pedra Branca (White Stone). To get there one has to go through a woods with a creek and crystalline ponds. Once out of the woods it's brute rock, carved out by wind and water through the millennia. The triumph of the rock? On rocks you cannot plant flowers. But life has built up organic matter in crevices and depressions. And now what you see is a garden: moss, orchids, bromeliads, maidenheads. If there were only rock, it would be desolation, desert. But life prospered on the rock, and then came the birds, the butterflies and the bees, the animals. Poor rock! Complaining is useless. Life and beauty grow on it in spite of its stony sameness. The seeds are stronger than the hard rock.

Then I understood something I had never understood before: the reason the Catholic Church chose for herself the symbol *petrus*. «You are the rock». Indeed she is a rock. A cicada's shell on a tree trunk, continuing to affirm itself, living on memories of the life that once was but now is death. She does not realize that life departed and flew away. I understood as well the reasons for her reluctance to deal with everything that has to do with seed —semen— the liquid of pleasure that makes one life come from another.

In the biblical story of Lot and his wife running away from Gomorrah, it is said that God ordered them not to look back. Lot's wife disobeyed. She looked back. She became a statue of salt. The rain and the wind wore away the salt. The statue disappeared. This is the tragedy of the stones: they believe they are eternal. They don't know that they are salt. Time does its work. Once upon a time the sand on the beach was stone.

Part Four

Tranquility

Tending sheep

89

Sunday morning. After much rain the sky was blue. Blue sky after lots of rain, is happiness. I'll take my flock to pasture. I invite my friend Alberto Caeiro to accompany me. Like me, he is a guardian of sheep. «My soul is like a shepherd's soul», he says.

> It knows the wind and the sun
> And walks hand in hand with the seasons
> Walking along and looking.
> All the peace of nature without people
> Comes to sit by my side.

If anybody calls him a liar, because he was never seen leading a flock, he promptly explains that, indeed, he does not guard bleating little lambs with white wool. His flocks are his ideas, which he leads on hikes through the countryside.

The countryside is good not only for sheep but also for ideas, especially on a day in which the outdoors is beautiful, but it's a little dark inside —a day that casts upon me a shadow of sadness. But my companion soon comforts me, saying that such

> sadness is quietness,
> Because it is natural and fair,
> And is what must be in the soul
> When it already thinks that it exists
> And without its awareness, hands collect flowers.

There I go, happy with my sadness, leading my visibly agitated flock. I think they caught the scent of a wolf in the air.

I gaze at the field. I feel that autumn is arriving. Its signs are unmistakable. First we have the air, which remains cooler, almost cold. A breeze blows by, in a game of trying to make the leaves twinkle in the sunlight. In the leaves of the eucalyptus it takes a bath of perfume, and comes to tickle the nose and the body hairs, which ruffle with pleasure. Enjoyable little coolness. From there it jumps to the molasses grass, shaking its flowery stems. Autumn's blossoms, for me, are prettier than the flowering of spring. Spring's blossoms are «because of». Autumn's are «in spite of».

I find the flowers of molasses grass a thousand times prettier than roses. Roses are domesticated entities. They are like the milk of cows in a corral, those huge cows, protected against sun and rain, with their huge motionless eyes, submissive, never thinking a forbidden thought, only knowing how to eat, regurgitate, give birth, and to produce milk that is sold in little plastic bags. Roses are like that, grown in greenhouses, not knowing what nature is really like, sometimes rough, sometimes playful —protected against sun and rain, all looking alike, all beautiful and empty.

The flowers of the molasses grass, on the other hand, are wild flowers. All efforts to domesticate them are useless. Upon feeling any human touch they collapse. They would rather die than be placed in a vase. The flowers of the grass are pretty only when in freedom, touched by the breeze, by the sun, by the gaze of the eye.

I don't have the happiness of my friend Alberto Caeiro, for whom only those who do not think see correctly. He says that thinking is an illness of the eyes. I understand and agree. It would be good to be able to gaze upon the countryside, with thoughts of nothing else. In the countryside one finds trees, breezes, blue sky, clouds, creeks, insects, birds. Have you ever seen any kind of anxiety walking through the countryside? Or any wrath sailing side by side with the clouds? Or any fear chirping like the birds? Never. These things do not exist in the countryside. They only exist in one's head. Thus, if my thoughts were identical to what I see, hear, smell and feel, walking through the countryside, my inner world would be like the outer world, and my mind would have the quiet simplicity of nature. I would have the same happiness as the gods, because, as my companion whispered to me in a moment of theological excitement, in gods the inner is identical to the outer. They do not have the unconscious. Therefore they are happy.

I don't have that happiness. I see and think. I remember Jesus's advice that we should look at the flowers of the field.

I looked, and they began to talk. And what did they say? They said what they always say, even when I am not there: «Your eyes look upon what has been happening for thousands of years. For thousands of years we have blossomed as we do now. For another thousand years we will continue to blossom. Many perturbed flocks, like yours, have passed by here. But we have no memories of them. They went and never returned. They disappeared in the River of Time. The River of Time makes all things disappear. Therefore nothing matters. Our anxieties are also destined for the River. They also will disappear in its waters. Your suffering comes from this, that you feel you are very important and do not pay attention to the voice of the River. When we believe we are important, we become too great. And, alongside the size of our importance, the size of our pain also grows. The River makes us small and humble. When that happens our pain diminishes. If you get to be small and humble like us, you will notice that we are part of a great symphony. Each grass, each creek, each cloud, each owl, each person is part of a Universal Harmony. The one who said this was Jesus. He said that for us to free ourselves of anxiety, we need to become as humble as the birds and the flowers».

Then my friend Alberto Caeiro intervened again:

When Spring arrives,
If I am already dead,
The flowers will blossom as they always do
And the trees won't be less green than in past Springs.
Reality does not need me.
I feel an enormous joy,
In thinking that my death doesn't matter at all.

I was frightened by these words, but he calmed me: «If you think that you are very important, then everything will depend on you. But, if you feel yourself to be humble, then all will depend on something greater than you. You will be, finally, in the arms of a Father, or in the lap of a Mother. And whoever is in the Father's arms, or in the Mother's lap, can sleep in peace».

Then the flowers of the grass spoke up: «The winter comes. And with it the cold and the drought. It will look as if I'm dead. But my seeds will have already been scattered. The spring will return, and with it, the joy of children and games. It is there in the Scriptures: "Send your bread upon the waters, for after many days you will get it back (Eccl.11:1)". Sounds like sheer nonsense. Bread once thrown upon waters disappears, and never comes back. But this is exactly what happens in the River of Time. The River is circular. What was lost returns. What keeps coming is what once was».

I looked around and saw my flock tenderly lying under a tree.

Angels

I have never seen an angel. Eyes that see angels are a special gift from the gods, not granted to all. I am not one of those who received it. But the gods granted me another organ to detect the angels: the nose. My nose is my angelical organ. I don't see angels. I smell them. For me, angels are olfactory beings. They reveal themselves to me through perfumes. I stroll down the street, deep in my thoughts. Suddenly, and unexpectedly, a fragrance fills my soul. I feel myself becoming light, losing solidity, and growing wings on my back, as I am immediately transported to an I-don't-know place where I once was happy. That lost happiness comes back to me. Since the occurrence is not the result of my initiative, I believe it's appropriate for me to imagine that the culprit is a perfumed angel, a friend of mine.

My angelical education began very early. I had my first lesson in a barbershop. There I saw an illustrated calendar that soothed and moved all who saw it; a bucolic landscape, a little boy and a little girl, unaccompanied shoeless siblings, strolling through a woods, about to cross a narrow plank bridge over a cliff: an impending fall. But no reason to fear. They were protected by an angel of muscular beauty with huge white wings. With a painting like that on the wall, fathers and mothers could sleep in peace. That was the Guardian Angel who, as far as I know, continues to guard children on bridges in the woods.

In the shop of a Syrian, I learned about angel feet. A humble customer came to the counter and asked: «Angel's feet, size 29, please».

Senhor Nagib promptly attended to the customer, selling him a pair of what today we call tennis shoes. Angel's feet were tennis shoes. It is easy to know why. The greatest pride of devout Catholic parents was to see their little daughter as part of a procession, dressed as an angel —a terrifying event for the ducks whose feathers were mercilessly plucked out to make the wings of the heavenly being. Their protestations were useless: ducks have no guardian angel. White garland, white wings, white dress, and, of course, white shoes as well —angel's feet.

Then, the teaching at the Sunday school of the Protestant church I attended. I was instructed to sing a hymn that said: «I want to be an angel/ an angel of dear God/ and imitate on earth the angels up in heaven». It was then that my vocation for heresy was triggered. For me the hymn was wrong: if God had made me a boy it was because God wanted me to be a boy. Therefore the hymn was a rebellion against the divine will. God wanted me to be a boy, and religious folk wanted me to be an angel. I did not want to be an angel, because I believed that an angel's life was very boring.

Eventually, I deepened my angelological knowledge by reading the poets. A poem by Fernando Pessoa says:

What angel, when you lifted up
Your voice unaware,
Came down
Over this land

Where the soul wanders,
And with its wings,
Blew on the live coals
Of a forgotten home?

The poet knew that lost homes are not really lost. They are guarded by angels who live in memory. There, the forgotten homes, like live coals, stay hidden under the ashes of forgetfulness. From time to time the angels ruffle their wings, blow the ashes, and the coals become fire. Psychoanalysis knows about this, although it shies away from calling angels by their real names, and instead comes up with other names.

Rilke was my other teacher. For him angels are terrifying entities, unlike the one who guided the two tender children in the woods. His *Duino Elegies* begins with an invocation of deaf angels:

Who, if I cried out, would hear me amid legions of Angels?
And even if one of them pressed me unexpectedly to his heart,
I would be consumed in that overwhelming existence.
For Beauty is nothing but the onset of terror
That we can scarcely endure,
and we are awed because it serenely disdains to annihilate us.
Every Angel is terrifying.

This poem is replete with mysteries that we cannot investigate here, given the limitation of space. Suffice it, for now, to hear the fearful exclamation: «Every Angel is terrifying!»

Isaac's son, Jacob, would agree with that. Pure fear from head to toe. He was walking along the road, invoking the protection of the Guardian Angel. It was a dark night. And there came the Angel —a terrible one, sword in hand. «Defend yourself, or I'll kill you», the Angel said. Jacob had no choice. He unsheathed his sword and fought the Angel, the whole night. And, amazingly, he won. At dawn, before departing, the Angel said: «I was defeated, but I'll leave you a souvenir, that you may not forget». Suddenly, he touched Jacob's thigh with his sword, and Jacob was lame for the rest of his life. He never forgot the incident. His lameness reminded him of it, at each step, and he felt emboldened. Never again was he afraid. He even had to change his name to Israel: «the one who fought with God and prevailed». Sometimes one has to fight with the Angel the whole night in order to acquire a name, to discover the real truth, a truth buried under ashes of fear.

But the angels that I really like are those who visited Jacob's grandparents, Abraham and Sarah. Abraham was already a toothless, emaciated old man, far distant from the pleasures of love. As for Sarah, his wrinkled, old wife with sagging breasts, her only remaining pleasures were the pleasures of the kitchen. And she was cooking for two guests when she heard the conversation in the living room. One of them was saying nonsensical things. Certainly he had drunk too much. He was saying that Sarah would become pregnant and have a baby. Sarah had an attack of laughter —she laughed so much that she burned the stew she was cooking. The guests took offense, and, as a punishment, said that the son would be called Isaac, which means «laughter».

These are the «Angels of Impossible Things». They are the ones that resurrect the dead, impregnate virgins, cause fountains to spring up in the desert, make trees blossom in the snow, touch old people with their swords, and make unexpected things happen.

What a delightful perfume! And what a sudden pain in my thigh! I think an angel passed nearby! But I'm not entirely sure. And while doubt endures, I'll fly a kite.

3

Corpus Christi

I am afraid of dying and going to heaven. I would feel out of place there. The poet Cecilia Meireles felt the same way. She wondered what happens…

> after one sails away
> to a certain place, and at last, arrives there…
> — Which would be, perhaps, sadder.
> Neither boat nor seagulls:
> only superhuman companions…

I need boats and seagulls too, because I love the sea and the air. I am an earthling and I believe that in my body there are rivers, trees, mountains and clouds. No hereafter could comfort me for losing them. Certainly a spirit, no matter how blessed, cannot smell the good scent of the molasses grass (which just opened its purple blossoms in the fields). For that it would need a nose. Neither would it be able to feel the cold, face-punishing wind on wintry evenings. It appears that spirits have no skin. And (poor things!) they can never feel the pleasure of diving in the sea. These animal pleasures are not available to spirits, those ethereal beings that, as far as we know, are immune to the effects of gravity. Their buoyancy protects them from falling off walls, but deprives them of the joy of diving. As soon as they jump they float in the air.

I love this world. That's why I don't want to go to heaven. Nietzsche felt the same. He even dreamed about the «perpetual return» —I will always return to this same place, the only one I know, of everyday material things that go from breakfast in the morning, coffee with milk and buttered bread, to the starry skies in the evening. Not to mention the pleasures of love, which cannot happen without the body. Indeed such pleasures require the enchantment of the eyes saying: «It's so good that you exist». And they need the sense of smell to perceive the perfume of the lilac. And what about the sense of hearing? What about the ancient serenades and poems of the «I love you» kind? They are all material things that cannot exist without the physics of speaking. I can't imagine a spiritual chant, although it is said that the cherubs play the harp and sing. Sounds need drums, trombones, violins, fingers, breathing, the body: they are physical and bodily things. I worry about the destiny of Bach and Beethoven as spirits forever, in the heavens, away from the good earthly instruments on which they played their music.

That's why I enjoyed the feast with the Latin name of *Corpus Christi*, an occasion on which, stubbornly and unconsciously, Christendom celebrates the body of Christ. If it had been the celebration of his soul, I confess I would have avoided it. Souls from the other world, whether good or evil, are dreadful apparitions.

But Corpus Christi Day, according to tradition, means that God, tired of being a spirit, not only discovered that nothing was as good as having a body, but also became incarnated, according to the witness of the apostles. God chose to be born as a body, in spite of all the risks, including the risk of dying. That's because the joys were a tradeoff. Thus God was born, which means that the body is eternally destined to a divine reality. Isn't it curious that humans prefer heaven while God prefers the earth? I remember the astonishment of the Indian chief who wrote to the President of the United States, saying that he couldn't understand why white people wished to live, after death, far away from earth. As for us, he said, we need the perfume of the pine-trees, the noise of water, the creeks, the twinkling of light on the surface of the lakes.

Corpus Christi: divine is the bread and all the earth where it grew, the water that made it germinate, the wind that caressed it, and the fire that baked it. Divine is the wine, sheer joy that gives the body wings and makes it float in the air. Things of the body: the whole universe fits inside it. It is not by chance that tradition speaks not of the immortality of the soul, but of the resurrection of the body. This is an affirmation that life is beautiful and that the divine is found in the simplest material things. As William Blake said: «To see a world in a grain of sand». Or the poet Fernando Pessoa: «All matter is spirit». Thus, I eat and drink the things of this world, the body of God.

4

Laudate Pueri

People praise as best they can. The rich magi brought expensive presents that they bought in crystal shops. The poor shepherds brought things that they had gathered with their own hands: the shine of the stars on silent nights, the music of the flutes in the loneliness of the hills, the scent of the grass wet with dew. The cows and mules, who couldn't buy or gather anything, praised the child with their tender look, and musically, in binary rhythm, with the swinging of their tails.

I also worship as best I can. It's five o'clock in the morning. In the middle of the sky, the moon, in the shape of a shining D, performs, quietly, its ministry of lighting. I think about you, whom I never saw, you who don't think about me, because you don't know I exist. I ask myself what kind of praise I know. Music, of course. There is nothing deeper. There are no words in the soul, the place never reached by perturbed human voices, where all is silent. Only music exists there. As for the physicists of today, the more they learn the sillier they become. They forget the wisdom of the ancients. They say that at the beginning of all things lies energy. Now I ask you, who never went to school: which comes first, the music or the instrument? Any fool knows that the music came first. Humans first heard music with the ears of the soul. And they were so fascinated that they began inventing instruments so that the body's ears could listen to it as well. Matter is born from music.

The ancient physicists knew about this. They looked up at the starry skies and heard the silent music of the spheres. Each star was a crystal globe, an instrument of an orchestra by which God played God's music. The evangelist wrote: «In the beginning was the Word». But, distracted as he was, he forgot to say that this Word was the lyrics of a song. He paid attention only to the letters. Otherwise he would have written: «In the beginning was the Music».

Since the universe begins again with your arrival, I thought it would be appropriate to combine the darkness of the night, the shine of the moon, and my blessed loneliness at dawn, with music; with the purpose of praising you. I don't want to give you only the music that exists in the gaps between my words. I want to offer you pure music. And so it was that I searched and found, among my CD's, the «*Laudate Pueri*» (Worship the Child), with harmonies by George Frederick Handel, Dietrich Buxtehude, Antonio Vivaldi. And this is what I listened to, while I wrote.

If you pay attention, you will perceive that your name is music —minimal music. It's enough to repeat out loud, Ana Carolina, Ana Carolina, Ana Carolina —a little ballerina who dances in slow motion, in binary rhythm— or would it be the flapping of a seagull's wings, also in binary rhythm? —maybe there is no difference— what all ballerinas want is to fly like birds, and that's why they jump so high, as if beseeching the gods for the miracle of transforming dance into flight —they want levitate, to float in the air.

A binary rhythm such as tum-tum, tum-tum, tum-tum, the beat of your mother's heart, on which your ears rested for nine months. You heard it so much that it became part of your little body, which now knows that when this rhythm is heard the universe is functioning in an orderly way. Tum-tum, tum-tum, tum-tum, nothing to fear, go to sleep. That's the rhythm of a lullaby, of a cradle, of hands patting the baby's behind. All trying to imitate the mother's heart.

I'm going to tell you a secret. It's a conversation between grandpa and granddaughter —parents not included. Don't tell them anything. Learn this: grownups are fools. It's important for you not to turn out to be like them. Of course, they will do all they can to pass you through the xerox machine called school. You should resist it. If I am still around, I'll help you. Take my word for it. Ask your little cousin, Mariana, about this. She will confirm what I'm saying.

The Little Prince… I forgot to ask if you, on your long trip to this earth, came across him? What is he like? It's easy to know. He lives in a minuscule asteroid, takes care of a rose, has a little lamb, and dies laughing when he thinks of grownups. He perceived what only we children perceive: that the grownups are all crazy. For example, he told me: if we tell the grownups that our house is white, with red windows, with a flower garden and birds on the roof, they look at us, scared, as if we were from another world. Now, if we tell them that we live in a three hundred thousand dollar house, they smile and say: «O, what a beautiful house!»

Grownups think that the biggest and the most expensive things are the best. They think that joys and gods come in big packages. For instance, when they talk about God, they are thinking about something big, very big, terrifying, something the size of the universe, and they keep talking about things that our thoughts cannot understand, such as time in billions of years, and distance in light years. They don't understand that the joyful, the wonderful, the divine, is just here at the reach of our hands. The divine is a dew drop, a purple mulberry, the mockingbird's dance, a sunbeam on a cobweb, the color of a lady-bug, a chocolate candy, a marble, a friend, a hit in a ball game, little things, priceless. Like you. You are very tiny, you are not worth very much on the market. But you are more marvelous than the whole universe. Because you have the power to give joy and to feel joy. The universe doesn't have this power. God is joy. A child is joy. God and a child have this in common: both know that the universe is a box full of toys. God sees the world with the eyes of a child. God is always looking for playmates. The big guys, the crazy ones, the perverse ones, think that God is like one of them, with wicked eyes, spying on them everywhere they go, to punish them. You know it is not like that.

Your little mouth on your mother's breast. Unaware of anything, you already know an essential philosophy: in the breast is a summary of everything worth knowing. First, that it is important to live. Milk gives life. But the breast is not only the place of milk. It is also the place of delight. The place of pleasure. We live for pleasure.

At the breast one learns that living is good. Living is divine. The world is a body full of breasts, a space full of paradises. But breasts and paradises only appear to those who have the eyes of a child.

These things I'm telling you are things that I rightly learned only after I became a grandfather. I knew about them when I was a child. But once I grew up, I became a serious person and forgot. After I became an old man, I forgot the things of grownups and relearned the things I had forgotten.

You know, Ana Carolina, I'm building a house for my grandchildren: you, Mariana and Camila, and others who may be coming. In that house I'm placing all my things for children, all my toys. They are the only things I find worth keeping. There you will find tops, marbles, kites, kaleidoscopes, puzzles, dolls, marionettes, a world of useless things that have the power to make dreams, story books, poetry books, song books, picture books, little gardens, fountains, plants, bonsais, paintings, posters, CD's. This is my house, my legacy: a house of toys for you. Now that you have arrived, even before seeing your face I look at my toys and imagine you playing with them. This makes me happy. And, who knows, even your parents and other grownups, turned children, may join us.

A big kiss from your grandpa and playmate.

Part Five

Beauty

1

The magi

Gaspar was king of Marrakesh, a country of blue sea and white shores. It was inhabited by men and women with light skin, black hair and brown eyes. To its coasts came ships from all over the world to sell their exotic merchandise. There was business everywhere —in the big plazas of the marketplace and in the small shops in narrow alleys. From the window of his palace, Gaspar beheld all that. Being the king, he should have been happy: everybody was thankful to him and everybody loved him. But, even so, there was an incurable sadness in his heart, a kind of nostalgia which was more deeply felt when the sun set over the sea, filling the waters with fire.

No matter how hard he tried, the king couldn't smile. Gaspar called his wise counselors to a meeting and told them about his sufferings. The wise counselors told him that the medicine for sadness was knowledge. «Science is a fountain of joy», they told him. The king then invited professors and scientists from all over the world, ordered books, established libraries, built laboratories, set up celestial observatories. For many years he devoted himself to learning science. Now he was old. He had learned everything he could learn about the world. But science didn't bring him joy. He still didn't know how to smile.

It was almost dawn. The sun had already lighted up the horizon. The king was awake. From the veranda of his palace he gazed at the starry sky. Then he turned his gaze to the East, and saw a new star, a star that didn't show in the celestial maps he had mastered. It was a different kind of star, because when he gazed at it, he heard music of infinite beauty, which made him happy. For the first time ever he smiled. Bedazzled, he ordered that the wise counselors be waked up and brought to him. He showed them the stars. They looked where the king pointed, but didn't see the star or hear the music that he said he was hearing. They left the palace commenting, sadly, on how old the king seemed; the years of senility were, finally, upon him. Gaspar, unconcerned about the incredulity of the wise counselors, ordered a ship prepared for a great voyage, in the direction of the star.

Balt-hazar was king of Nubia, a mountainous country of men and women with black and shining skin. Nubia's mountains were covered with luxurious vegetation, all kinds of giant fruit trees that housed birds of all sorts. All over the country one saw creeks of clear water, calm pools and waterfalls. It was a beautiful and fertile land. From the window of his palace, Balt-hazar looked upon the mountains and forests, which stretched far beyond the reach of the eyes: «The original paradise must have been this place».

However, in spite of the beauty and fertility of the land, the king was not happy. There was a sadness in his heart, a sadness that grew deeper when the birds chirped their songs at sunset. Their chirping was beautiful and sad.

The king called his priests, seers and prophets, and told them about his sadness. «What's the use of the beauty of my country, if my heart is sad?» he asked. The holy group told him that his sadness was a sign that his soul was distant from God. «God is a source of joy», they told him. Balt-hazar then invited, from far away lands, mystics and theologians who could teach him the ways to God. He also brought in architects and artists to build new temples. Further, he bought sacred books from all the religious traditions in the world. And, for many years, he devoted himself to sacred living: he read, meditated and prayed. At last, old age was upon him. Balthazar knew everything that anyone knew about the ways to God. But his heart remained sad; and even more so, when the birds sang at the end of the day.

It was already dawn. Balt-hazar, as usual, woke up early to pray. He was gazing at the sky, the place of the gods. It was then that, looking at the horizon where the sun rose, he saw a star he had never seen before. Surrounding it was a rainbow. But the strange thing was that when he gazed at the star, he heard music of enormous beauty, like the songs of birds at the end of the day. The difference was that, when he heard it, he didn't become sad. On the contrary; he was overwhelmed with a joy such as he had never before experienced.

The king called the priests, mystics and prophets to his palace. «Look at that star», he said, pointing to the horizon. «And listen to the music coming from it!» The holy group looked where he was pointing, but neither saw the star or nor heard the music. They left the king inebriated with joy, and whispered among themselves: «Our king is out of his senses. This means that his life is coming to an end». But Balt-hazar ordered horses prepared for a long trip, in the direction of the star.

Mélek-hor was king of Lagash, a country of wilderness and endless sands, of women with almond shaped eyes and wild bearded men. His joys were the oases scattered over the sandy plains with the green of their palm trees and the coolness of their fountains. It was in one of these oases that Mélek-hor built his palace, in the shape of a pyramid, from huge blocks of white stones. Pyramids, as is well known, are magic shapes that ensure immortality.

He didn't mind the dryness and solitude of desert life. In fact, he took them as a challenge for both body and soul. But there was something that made him suffer: an indefinable melancholy that he felt when gazing upon the horizons of waving sands colored red by the setting sun.

The king invited his friends to dinner, and told them about his melancholy. They told him: «This is understandable. Our country is very dry. What you are missing, dear king, are the pleasures of life. Pleasures will make you smile». Mélek-hor, then ordered pleasures from all over the world: wines, fruits, delicacies, musicians, artists, beautiful women. For years he devoted himself to these pleasures. In this nobody surpassed him. But the pleasures didn't bring him joy. And he, already old, prayed in silence: «I don't want pleasures; I want joy».

The dawn's light announced the coming end of the night. The king, at the top of his pyramid, had a glass of wine. It was his habit to watch the rising sun; this always gave him pleasure. But the pleasure of beauty always came to him mingled with sadness. This time, however, he didn't feel any sadness. He was surprised to find that he was joyful. And the joy came from a new star that had never been seen before. And —strange!— watching it, he heard a melody that filled him with happiness. Mélek-hor then smiled for the first time. Bedazzled, he called his friends to the palace. He pointed to the star and told them about the music. But they, looking at the sky, neither saw the star nor heard the music. Since they were good friends, they told the king: «Dear Mélek-hor, our beloved king, there is no star or music. Your mind doesn't perceive earthly things any more. It sails over the great river toward the third bank. We cry because we know that you will be departing». And, sadly, they left, singing a quiet requiem. But the king, quite unconcerned about the words of his friends, ordered camels prepared for a journey in the direction of the star.

Gaspar, coming from the North in his ship, Balt-hazar, coming from the South on his horse, Mélek-hor, coming from the West on his camel: three kings who didn't know each other. Now each one, from his place, began a journey in the direction of a star that only they could see, and of a music that only they could hear.

Gaspar sailed in his boat. But in a storm it crashed against the reefs and sank. The king, carried by the waves to the shore, continued his journey on foot: the seaman turned a pedestrian. And it so happened that, after a long walk, he arrived at a crossroad where the four roads of the world met: one from the North, one from the South, one from the West, and the fourth, which led to the star in the East. It was at the inn that the three voyagers met. They discovered, then, that they were brothers: they all came from the same nostalgia, and they all came in search of the same joy.

Then they continued the journey together until they reached a village. «What village is this?» they asked. «Bethlehem»: this was its name, carved on a rock. «Strange», said Gaspar, «I've learned all that is to be learned about kingdoms, provinces, towns and villages. But never did I see this name in any of the books I read». Balt-hazar lighted his oil lamp and examined the map that he had opened on the ground. «Here it is», he said, pointing with his finger to a place on it. «Beth-lehem. Precisely on the border between two great kingdoms. On the left, the Kingdom of Fantasy. On the right, the Kingdom of Reality. These are dangerous kingdoms. Whoever lives in the Kingdom of Fantasy ends up insane. Whoever lives in the Kingdom of Reality ends up insane. To escape insanity one has to be always moving from one kingdom to the other. Because Beth-lehem lies on the border».

In the village all were sleeping. It was a peaceful night. The air was perfumed with the scent of jasmine and magnolia. And there was a radiance in the air —thousands, millions of fireflies perched on trees. And in the air, the sound of a shepherd's flute.

The star lighted a cave. The kings approached. In the cave were cows, horses, mules, sheep. It was a stable. But near the animals was a small family: a young man and a young woman nursing a newborn baby. That was all. Nothing more.

They saw that they had been mistaken: it was not the star that lighted up the scene. It was the little baby that lighted up the star. And looking up, they could see, reflected in the star, as in a mirror, the face of the little baby. And they said: «The universe is a crib where a child sleeps!»

Then something strange happened: every time they looked at the baby, they lost their usual composure. They were overwhelmed by an incredible desire to laugh. And when they laughed, they began to float. That's how it was: whoever saw the child became an angel.

The kings, amidst their laughter, looked at each other and said: «Our search has come to an end. We have found joy. In order to find joy, one has to become a child again». And, immediately, they took off their crowns, their velvet coats, their money, their gold and their jewels —those grownup things— and placed them on the ground beside the cows and mules. Those things were too heavy. And they departed light, sometimes walking, sometimes jumping, sometimes flying, but always smiling.

«I'm going to change my life», said Gaspar. «It's awful to be studying science all the time. I'm going to become a poet».

«Me too», said Balt-hazar. «It's awful to be praying all the time. I am going to be a clown. Laughter is the beginning of prayer».

To this Mélek-hor added: «I have discovered the supreme pleasure, which is always accompanied by joy: to play. I'm going to be a toymaker. Whoever plays becomes a child again. And whoever becomes a child is back in paradise».

And there they went, each his own way. If you, on your pilgrimage, happen to meet a poet, or a clown or a toymaker, ask them if they have any news of the three kings.

A mystical experience
is seeing the world
through beauty.

2

Outside beauty there is no salvation

I write as a poet. Cummings said that the boundless world of the poets is the poets themselves. Egocentric narcissism? Not necessarily. I turn to Cecília Meireles to clarify this point. She said in a poem to her grandmother: «Your body is a thinking mirror of the universe». Poets —unlike scientists who want to know the universe by looking directly at it— know the universe only as part of their bodies. Poetry is the Eucharist. The poet contemplates it and says: «This is my body».

Being a poet, I don't know how to talk scientifically about Christianity. I can only talk about it as it is reflected in the mirror of my body, through time.

Childhood. Children don't have religious ideas. They know nothing of spiritual entities. Children are creatures of this world. They experience it through their senses, especially through sight. Children don't have religious ideas, but they have mystical experiences. A mystical experience is not a vision of beings from other worlds. It is seeing this world illuminated through beauty. It is a grand experience, and beyond language. Religious feelings arise from this kind of experience.

Religion is the empty shell of the cicada on the stem of a tree. Religious feeling is the cicada in flight. As a child, I flew with the cicadas.

Religious ideas don't originate with children. They are placed on the bodies of children by grownups. My mother taught me to pray: «Now I lay me down to sleep. I pray the Lord my soul to keep. If I should die before I wake, I pray the Lord my soul to take. Amen». This is a minimalist summary of Christian theology: there is a God, there is death, there is a soul that survives death. Then other lessons followed: «God is looking at you». God turns out to be a Big Eye that sees everything and watches me. My first feeling related to God was fear.

Children believe what grownups tell them. Thus begins an education process through which grownups proceed to write on the bodies of children the words of religion. The child's body ceases to be the child's body; it becomes a notebook where grownups write their religious words.

Many are the lessons of the catechism. God is a spirit who knows all things. He sees what you are doing with your hands, under the blanket, in the dark. God is omnipotent: God can do anything. God has absolute power, and everything that happens is the result of his will. Handicapped children, a mother who dies in childbirth, torture chambers, wars. Tragedies do not happen. God produces them. In the face of tragedies one is taught to repeat: «This is God's will». I have to do what God orders, otherwise God will punish me. If I die without repenting, I will be eternally punished with the fire of hell. This earthly life in the body has no value. This is a valley of tears, where the children of the exiled Eve lament and cry, waiting for heaven. Heaven comes after death. God lives in that after death place. The world is a minefield of pleasures where the soul's eternal destiny will be decided. In order to love God, one has to hate life. Whoever loves the good things of life does not love God. One has to deny the body: lacerations, abstentions, and sacrifices are gifts one should offer to God. God is happy when we suffer. Of all pleasures, the most dangerous are the pleasures of sex. Therefore, sex must be performed without pleasure. Sex is for procreation. God has never been seen by anyone, but God's will was revealed to an institution: the Church, whether Catholic or Protestant. To this institution, the Church, was entrusted the book written under divine inspiration, the Holy Scriptures, the «Great Encyclopedia of Knowledge and Divine Orders». Therefore, «outside the Church there is no salvation», because outside the Church there is no knowledge of God.

Ludwig Wittgenstein talks about the spellbinding power of words. Words are spellbinding: they overpower us and prevent us from thinking. Religious ideas are like this: people's bodies are covered with words that overpower them through fear. Once «possessed», they are unable to think different thoughts. Any word other than these may mean hell. The Catholic and Protestant inquisitions never sent people to the fire for their moral sins. Moral sins keep people close to the Church, because she has the power to forgive. The only ones who burned in its fire were those whose thoughts were different: Bruno, Huss, Servetus. Crimes of thought distract people from the Church. Consequently they distract people from God. Whoever thinks different thoughts must be eliminated either by fire or by silence.

For many years I lived spellbound by these words. Spellbinding cannot be undone by reason. It is always a kiss of love that breaks the spell. Who kissed me? One who lives in me. Because in me lives not only the one who thinks, but also the one who feels. Roland Barthes said: «…my body does not have the same ideas I do». I was thinking the words that had been written on my body. But my body thought other ideas. The truth of my body was another truth. My body loved life too much. I must confess: I was never attracted by the delights of heaven. I don't know anyone who is dying of love for them. The proof of this is that people take good care of their health. They want to stay here. But I know people with tortured lives, because of their fear of Hell.

I remember precisely the moment I had the intellectual perception that freed my reason to think. I was at the Seminary. Suddenly, astonished, I perceived that all those words that other people had written on my body had not fallen from heaven. If they had not fallen from heaven, they had no right to be where they were. They were invading demons. My eyes opened and I perceived that this monumental architecture of theological words, which we call Christian theology, is all built around the idea of Hell. If Hell were eliminated, all the logical screws would loosen, and the great building would collapse. Orthodox Christian theology, both Catholic and Protestant —except for that of the mystics and heretics— is a description of the complicated mechanisms invented by God to save some people from Hell. The most extraordinary of these mechanisms is the act of an implacable Father who, instead of simply forgiving freely (as loving human fathers do), kills His only Son on a cross in order to balance his cosmic accounting. It is obvious that whoever invented this has never been a father. In the realm of love fathers are always the ones who die, so that their children may live.

Today, the central ideas of Christian theology, in which I used to believe, mean nothing to me: they are like the cicada shell, empty. They don't make any sense. I don't understand them. I don't love them. I can't love a Father who kills a Son to satisfy his justice. Who can? Who believes that?

Even more curious is the fact that I continue to be linked to this tradition. There is something in Christianity that is part of my body. I know it is not ideas. What is it, then?

It was on Good Friday that I understood this. An FM radio station was broadcasting, the whole day, music of the Christian religious tradition. And there I stayed, sitting, just listening. Suddenly, a mass by Bach. The beauty was such that I felt possessed, and cried from happiness: Beauty makes one cry. I perceived that such beauty was part of me. It could never be wrenched from my body. For centuries theologians, cerebral beings, had devoted themselves to transforming beauty into rational speech. Beauty was not enough for them. They wanted certainty, they wanted truth. However, artists, beings of the heart, know that the highest form of truth is beauty. Now, without any shame, I say: «I am a Christian, because I love the beauty that lives in this tradition. What about the ideas? They are the screech of static, in the background».

Therefore I proclaim the only dogma of my erotic-heretic Christian theology: «Outside Beauty there is no salvation».

Highest form of truth is beauty

The bet

We gathered and listened to the witnesses: psychologists, philosophers, social scientists. Some of them, on the side of the prosecution, testified that religion is a crazy thing that babbles senseless notions, spreading illusions, making alliances with the powerful, and narcotizing the poor. Others, testifying for the defense, affirmed that without religion the world cannot exist, and that when we decipher its symbols, we see ourselves as in a mirror. Furthermore, they said, it is exactly with such symbols that the oppressed build their hopes and fight on.

Curiously, none of these witnesses have ever been seen in sacred places, searching for communion with the divine. Even more serious is the fact that not a single one of them has ever believed in what religion says.

That's the way of the scientists. They pay attention without believing; they listen and take notes, convinced that humans don't know what they are talking about. They think that all those who haven't received a scientific education, all the common people, are like sleepwalkers: they move around surrounded by a cloud of illusions and errors that hinder their vision of the truth. They are shortsighted or blind. They see things upside-down. Not because of bad faith, but because of their cognitive incapacity. This is the reason why scientists listen with a condescending smile. It is up to them, the scientists, to extract from commonsensical speech the truth that only science can obtain. That is why no scientist can believe in the words of religion. If they did so, they would be religious people, not men or women of science.

They don't have any alternative. All sciences, without exception, are obliged to adopt a rigorous methodological atheism. Demons and gods cannot be invoked to explain anything. Everything happens, in the game of science, as if God didn't exist. If such is the starting point of scientists, how could they believe in God and be naive enough to pray?

But don't we have a duty of honesty that obliges us to listen to the voice of religion, which, so far, has been silent? Don't we have to allow it to articulate its point of view? Shall we behave like the inquisitors? In Alice's wonderland, there was a famous trial in which the judge [the Queen of Hearts] shouted: «Sentence first, verdict afterwards!» Will ours be the behavior of this crazy magistrate? No. We'll have to listen to the voice of religion, even if such a voice is closer to poetry than to science.

We have a strange and wonderful capacity to play at make-believe: the game of abandoning our certainties just to see the world's configuration with the eyes of another person. That's what we will have to do now, asking the scientists in us to be quiet, so as to allow, perhaps, a piece of ourselves to be heard—a piece that, without invoking sacred names, insists on desiring, on hoping, on expressing its silent cries of yearning and protest, through the bottomless moments of insomnia and suffering. Perhaps we don't believe in gods, but it may well be that we wish they existed. This would bring peace to our hearts. We would have certainty about the things that we love and that, sadly, we see aging, decaying and vanishing.

Ah! If only we could be impregnated by the gods! This is the way we cross to another world where talking is not subordinated to the eyes, but is linked to the heart. For «the heart has reasons that reason cannot know» (Pascal).

An old sorcerer told his apprentice that the secret of his art was in learning to make the world stop. Such advice sounds crazy, but it becomes wisdom when we realize that our world has been petrified by habit. We get used to talking about the world in a certain way. We always conceive of it inside the same frames, we always see everything the same way, and our feelings get jaded because we know that what is going to be is the same as what has been. But when we play make-believe, it is as if our world suddenly stopped, so that the language, thought, eyes and feelings of another person set forth a new world before us. This was what happened to the poor frogs in the following parable, which has already been told somewhere, and which I'm going to repeat here.

«In a place not very far away from here, there was a deep, dark pond where, since time immemorial, there lived a society of frogs. The pond was so deep that none of them had ever seen the outside world. They were convinced that the universe was the size of that hole. There was more than enough evidence to corroborate that theory, and only an insane person, deprived of reason, would dispute it. It so happened that a goldfinch, flying over that area, became curious and decided to investigate the depth of the pond. What a surprise for him to discover the frogs! The frogs were even more surprised, because that feathered creature raised doubts about all the truths that had been laid down and proven in their society for centuries. The goldfinch was sorry for them. How in the world could frogs live in such a pond, without any hope of getting out? Of course the idea of getting out was an absurdity to them, since, to them, that hole was the universe, and such a thing as an «out there» was an impossibility.

«The goldfinch began to sing furiously. It praised the soft breeze, the green fields, the crowned trees, the crystal clear creeks, the butterflies, the flowers, the clouds, the stars —and this caused a great commotion, and a split in the society of frogs. Some of them believed, and began to imagine what it would be like out there. They became more joyous and even prettier. They croaked new songs. Others frowned. Affirmations not confirmed by experience weren't trustworthy, they said. The goldfinch might be saying senseless things and spreading lies. Immediately they engaged in philosophical, sociological and psychological criticism of its speech. For whom was the goldfinch working? The ruling classes? The oppressed classes? Might its singing be a kind of narcotic? Was the bird insane? Was the bird deceitful? Was it possible that the bird was spreading a kind of collective hallucination? But

there was no denying that the chant had created many problems. Neither the ruling nor the ruled frogs (who secretly plotted a revolution) liked the ideas that the goldfinch was bringing to the common folk. When the goldfinch came back for a second visit, it was arrested, accused of deceiving of the people, killed, stuffed, and the croaking of the songs he taught was outlawed for ever».

That's how it happened: science snuffed out religion, taking from it truths very different from the truths sung by living religion itself. It so happens that religious people, in saying the sacred names, do indeed express their belief in an «out there», and the nourishment of their hopes comes from that invisible world. All so distant, so different from scientific wisdom.

If we are going to listen to religious people, we must pretend that we believe them. Is it possible that the goldfinch is right? Is it possible that the universe is prettier and more mysterious than the boundaries of our pond? What does religion talk about?

We shouldn't be distracted by the exuberance of symbols and gestures, coming from far and near, from the past and from the present, because the theme of the song is always the same. They are all variations of the fundamental melody. Religion talks about the meaning of life. It declares that life is worthwhile, that we can be happy and smile. And what all of them set forth is nothing less than a series of recipes for happiness. This is the reason why people continue to be fascinated with religion, in spite of all the criticism coming from science. Science sets us in a glacial and mechanical world, a mathematically and technically precise as well as manipulable world, but a world empty of human meaning and indifferent to love. Max Weber used to say that the hard lesson we learn from science is that the meaning of life cannot be found at the conclusion of a scientific analysis, no matter how complete it is. We find ourselves expelled from paradise, with the vestige of pedantry still in our hands.

The meaning of life: no other question is raised with deeper anxiety. It seems as if we are all haunted by it, from time to time. Is life worthwhile? The seriousness of the question is revealed in the seriousness of the answer. It is not rare for us to see people in the abyss of insanity, or voluntarily choosing the abyss of suicide, because they have received a negative answer. Other people, as Albert Camus observed, allow themselves to be killed by ideas and illusions that give them reasons to live: good reasons to live are good reasons to die.

But what kind of thing is the meaning of life?

The meaning of life is something that one experiences emotionally, without knowing how to explain or justify it. It is not something one builds, but something that occurs unexpectedly, without preparation, like a gentle breeze that touches us unexpectedly, without our knowing where it came from or where it is going. It is something that we experience as an intensification of our will to live, to the point of granting us the courage to die, if necessary, for those things that give life its meaning. It is the transformation of our vision of the world into one in which things become integrated, like a melody that makes us feel reconciled with the universe around us, and possessed by a boundless feeling —in the words of Romain Rolland— the indescribable sensation of eternity and infinity, of communion with something that transcends us, envelops us, and cradles us like a motherly womb of cosmic dimensions

> To see a world in a grain of sand
> and a heaven in a wild flower,
> hold infinity in the palm of your hand
> and eternity in an hour.
> — William Blake

The meaning of life is a feeling.

If the claims of religion stopped here, everything would be all right. For there are no laws that prohibit us from feeling whatever we want. The scandal begins when religion dares to transform such interior or subjective feelings into a hypothesis about the universe. We can understand why religious people are not satisfied with a lifeless bird. Religion says: «The whole universe makes sense». And science replies: «Religious people feel and think that the universe makes sense». That sacred affirmation, which echoed from universe to universe, resonating in eternities and infinities, is incarcerated by science in the small, dark pond of subjectivity and society: illusion, ideology. The meaning of life is destroyed. What will remain of the joy of the frogs, if the «out there» sung by the goldfinch does not exist?

To affirm that life has meaning is to propose a fantastic hypothesis that the universe vibrates with our feelings, suffers the pain of the tortured, sheds the tears of the abandoned and smiles with the children at play. Everything is linked. It's the conviction that behind visible things is an invisible smiling face, a friendly presence, arms that hug, as in the famous painting by Salvador Dali. This is the belief that explains the sacrifices offered on altars and the prayers whispered in solitude.

It is possible that such images have never gone through your head, and that you feel lost amidst the metaphors used by religious experience. I remember one of the deepest dialogues ever produced in world literature, in which Ivan Karamazov argues with his brother Aliosha, invoking the story of a little boy who had been punished by his parents for wetting his bed. The boy was locked in a small, dark and cold room, outside the house, on a freezing cold night. Aliosha describes the boy's little hands banging on the door, asking to be allowed to leave, while tears roll down his face, contorted by fear. What reasons, in the whole universe, could be invoked to explain and justify that pain? One feels that there is something deeply wrong here, eternally wrong, always wrong, with no mitigating circumstances, from the beginning to the end of the world. We feel the same, when we think of the tortured, of the executed, of those who die of hunger, of those enslaved, of those who ended their days in concentration camps, of animal lives destroyed by greed, of weapons, and of abandoned elderly people. We could multiply endlessly the number of similar cases.

What compelling reasons do we have to say «no» to such acts? Could it be simply our feelings? But, if that were the case, what could we say when the executioner, the torturer, the warmongers similarly invoke their feelings in defense of their actions? They also feel. Even they are human.

No, our ethical judgements are not anchored only in our feelings. It is true that we use them. But it is also true that we invoke the whole universe as a witness and guarantor of our cause. The heart's voice vibrates with the infinite. We believe that the universe has a human heart, a vocation for love, a preference for happiness and freedom —as we all do. This means that to announce that life has meaning is to proclaim that the universe is our sister and brother. And it is this reality, this anchor of feelings, that receives the name of God.

Religion took special care in building houses for the gods and houses for the dead, temples and tombs. There are no other beings in the world who raise their prayers to heaven and bury their dead with symbols, as we do. This is not accidental. Because death is the presence that, from time to time, touches us lightly and asks: «In spite of me, do you still believe that life makes sense?»

How does one explain the meaning of life when confronted by death? What kind of comfort can one offer the parent of a dead child? Should one say that the child's life was short, but beautiful? How does one comfort a person with a terminal illness, who sees affection and smiles drifting farther and farther away? And what about the millions who die unfairly: Treblinka, Hiroshima, Biafra?

All so different from a Mozart sonata: short and perfect. In twenty minutes, all that should be said is said. The final chord doesn't interrupt anything, it only completes it.

How to affirm the meaning of life in the face of the absurdity of existence, as represented by death reducing to nothing all that love built and expected?

«What is finite for the understanding is nothing for the heart» (Feuerbach). Here is the problem: «On one side the eternal star, and on the other the unpredictable wave». (Cecília Meireles). The meaning of life hangs on the meaning of death. Thus religion delivers its dead to the gods, in hope. Between the house of the gods and the house of the dead shines the hope of eternal life, so that humans may reconcile themselves with death and be free to live. When death is transformed into a friend, one doesn't have to struggle against it. Isn't it true that our whole life is a heedless struggle to push far away the «near and resourceless» horizons? Society is a group of people who go forward, although resisting, in the direction of inevitable death.

Think about what you would do, if you were told that you had only three months to live. After the initial panic… Your daily routine, the things that you consider important, not postponable, to which you sacrifice leisure, meditation and play… Reading the newspaper, checkbook stubs, income tax forms, the resentments of married life, professional hatreds, college graduation, career perspectives. All this would shrink to the point of almost disappearing. And the present would gain a dimension it never had before, of seeing and savoring each moment, because they are the last moments: the forgotten painting on the wall; the scent of jasmine; the singing of a bird, somewhere; the chirping of crickets before sleep arrives; the noise of children; the drops of cold water near the fountain. You might even get the courage to take off your shoes and go into the water. Why worry about scaring the upright folks?

Maybe we find here the reason why society hides and disguises death, even making it a forbidden topic of conversation. Awareness of death has the power to liberate, and this subverts the loyalties, values and considerations on which the social order depends. In placing the tombs in hands of the gods, religion forces the enemy to be transformed into a sister or a brother. Free to die, humans are free to live.

But the meaning of life is not a fact. In a world still under the sign of death, where the highest values are crucified, and where brutality triumphs, it is an illusion to proclaim harmony with the universe as the current reality. Therefore religious experience depends upon a future. It nourishes itself on utopian horizons that the eyes have never seen, and that can only be envisioned by the magic of imagination. God and the meaning of life are absences, realities one yearns for, gifts of hope. Indeed, hope may be the great badge of religion. Perhaps we may affirm, with Ernst Bloch: «Wherever there is hope, there is religion».

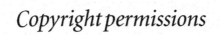 *Copyright permissions*

Our special thanks for the permission which was granted to us to reproduce the following essays of Rubem Alves:

«A aposta [The bet]». *O que é religião?* São Paulo: Loyola, 1999.

«A oração [Prayer]». *Festa de Maria.* Campina. SP: Papirus/Speculum, 1996.

«Anjos [Angels]». *As contas de vidro e os fios de nylon.* São Paulo: Ars Poética, 1997.

«As promessas [Promises]». *Festa de Maria.* Campina, SP: Papirus/Speculum, 1996.

«Corpus Christi». *Tempus fulgit.* São Paulo: Paulus, 2001.

«De novo, sobre o inferno [Again, about Hell]». *Coisas da alma.* São Paulo: Paulus, 2001.

«Deus existe? [Does God exist?]» *Teologia do cotidiano. Meditações sobre o momento e a eternidade.* São Paulo: Olho D'Água, 1994.

«Inferno [Hell]». *Coisas da alma.* São Paulo: Paulus, 2001.

«Laudate Pueri». *As contas de vidro e os fios de nylon.* São Paulo: Ars Poética, 1997.

«Meu Deus, me cura de ser grande [Dear God, cure me of being a grownup]». *As contas de vidro e os fios de nylon.* São Paulo: Ars Poética, 1997.

«O batisado [The baptized one]». *Sobre o tempo e a eternidade.* Campinas, SP: Papirus, 1995.

«O que amo na Igreja [What I love in the Church]». *Cenas da Vida.* Campinas, SP: Papirus/Speculum, 1996.

«Pastoreio [Tending sheep]». *As contas de vidro e os fios de nylon.*
São Paulo: Ars Poética, 1997.

«Sem contabilidade [Without accounting]». *As contas de vidro
e os fios de nylon.* São Paulo: Ars Poética, 1997.

«Sobre a salvação da minha alma [On the salvation of my soul]».
Coisas da Alma. São Paulo: Paulus, 2001.

«Vitral [The stained glass window]». *As contas de vidro e os fios
de nylon.* São Paulo: Ars Poética, 1997.

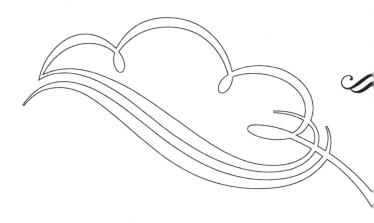

Transparencies of eternity

This book was printed on *thin opaque smooth white Bible paper*, using the *Minion* and *Type Embellishments One* font families.

This edition was printed in D'VINNI, S.A., in Bogotá, Colombia, during the last weeks of the sixth month of year two thousand ten.

Ad publicam lucem datus mense junii Sacri Cordis Iesus